LIVING TRADITIONS

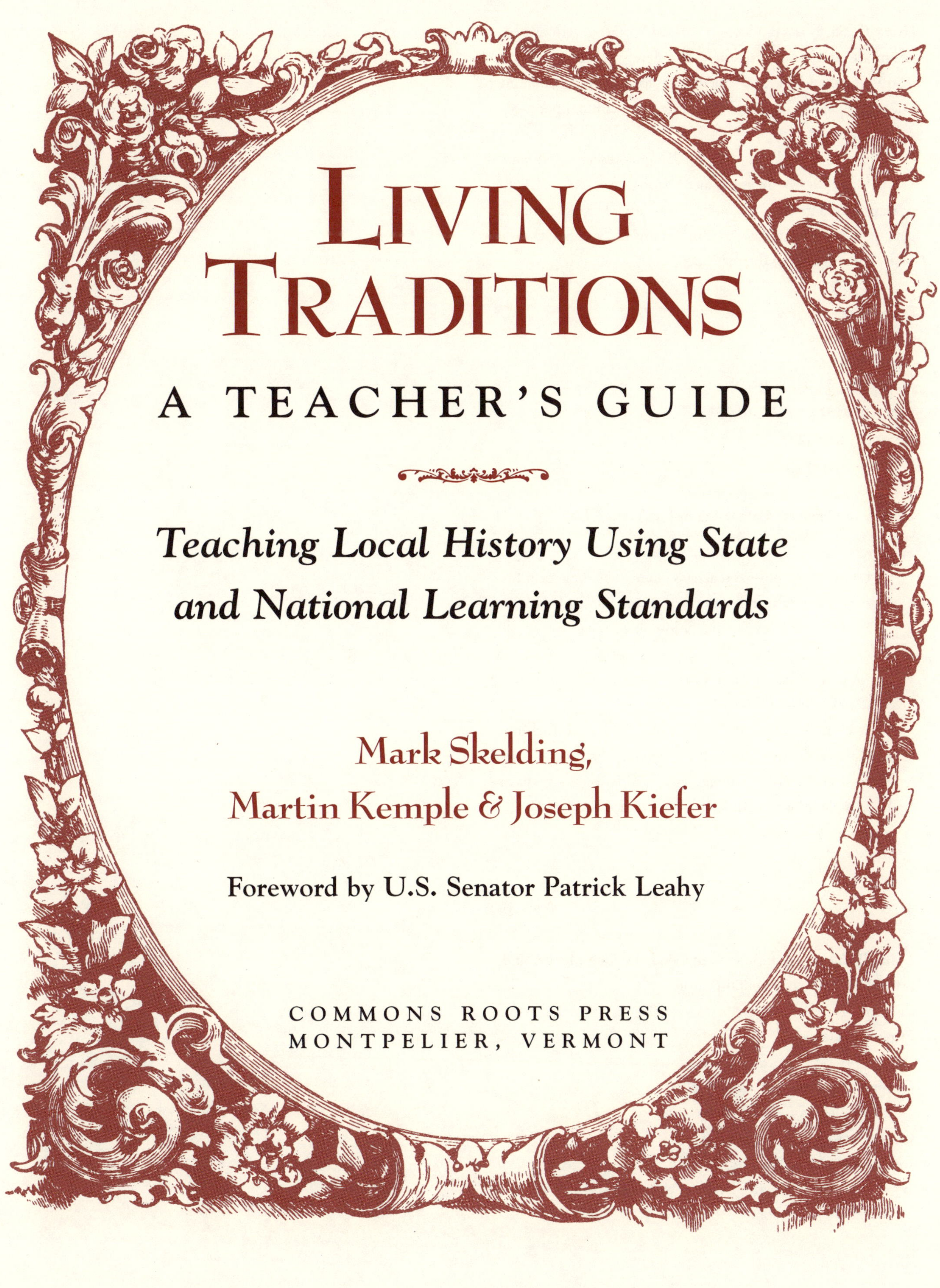

Living Traditions

A Teacher's Guide

Teaching Local History Using State and National Learning Standards

Mark Skelding,
Martin Kemple & Joseph Kiefer

Foreword by U.S. Senator Patrick Leahy

COMMONS ROOTS PRESS
MONTPELIER, VERMONT

Living Traditions is a production of Food Works, a Vermont-based nonprofit educational organization, offering courses, workshops, instructional videos, and guidebooks for creating community-based curricula focused on local natural and cultural heritage.

Food Works
Common Roots Press
64 Main Street
Montpelier, Vermont 05602
(802) 223-1515   800-310-1515
Fax (802) 229-5277
foodwork@together.net

Library of Congress Cataloging-in-Publication Data

Skelding, Mark.
Living traditions—a teacher's guide : teaching local history using state and national learning standards / Mark Skelding, Martin Kemple & Joseph Kiefer.
p. cm.
"A production of Food Works"—T.p. verso.
ISBN 1-884430-06-6
1. United States—History, Local—Study and teaching—Handbooks, manuals, etc. 2. Curriculum planning—United States—Handbooks, manuals, etc. I. Title: Living traditions. II. Kemple, Martin. III. Kiefer, Joseph. IV. Food Works (Organization) V. Title.
E175.8 .K34 2001
973'.071—dc21

00-065903

Living Traditions was formatted in Goudy by Kate Mueller and printed by Transcontinental Printing.

Printed in Canada.

Cover and text design: Kate Mueller / Electric Dragon Productions
Cover photograph: Joseph Kiefer
Illustrations: Mary Azarian
Book production: Electric Dragon Productions, Montpelier, Vermont

We dedicate this book to those peoples everywhere
who are living the traditions passed down
from generation to generation
in the day-to-day life of all communities.

These are the real leaders,
the numberless unknown heroes equal to the greatest heroes known,
who have stayed true to the well-worn but neglected footpaths
winding through our collective memory.

Acknowledgments

In writing this book about how to bring communities' natural and cultural heritage to life in schools, we readily acknowledge that our greatest debt is to history itself and to those who carry that history in their day-to-day lives, our elders.

Through our work, we have been blessed to be connected to a long list of elders who share our commitment to making the past meaningful in the lives of young people. Though their numbers are far more than we could list here, just a few of them include: Dolores "Ma" Roy, a fiesta octogenarian with strong French-Canadian and Native American roots who, since the early 1980s, has been sharing with us her life stories and experiences growing up in a large family and living off the land in a hard-scrabble rural community in Vermont's Northeast Kingdom. Thelma White, a retired schoolteacher, principal, and school board member who still carries an infectious excitement for the mysteries of nature as our greatest teacher—from birding to gardening and from hiking to singing—has shown us again and again how an elder can cross the generations with insight and wonder by sharing the stories of her life. And John Wires, a lifelong mentor whose "walking University" up mountain paths and over long-lost trails has shown us how to make the natural world and the understanding of nature's complex voices the ultimate teacher of our collective history on this planet.

The schools and communities that have been doing this work for decades are the true inspiration for compiling these activities, projects, and curriculum development strategies into one volume. Two Vermont schools in particular—the Peacham Elementary School and the Union School in Montpelier—have provided a learning laboratory to explore the central question of this book: How do we sustain the traditional skills and values unique to each place in a modern school system fixated on technology, progress, and the future? In Peacham, Principal Margaret McLean and teachers Sarah Parker and Lynn Talamini taught us how to make cultural literacy fit the curriculum. All of us in the Montpelier community owe particular thanks to Union Principal Jen Miller-Arsenault together with teachers Teresa Giffen, Patty Gaston, Bev Keck, Harriet Grenier, and, especially, Newton Baker, who have demonstrated throughout their careers a strong commitment to locally based curriculum that teaches the whole child.

Special thanks must also go to Julie Barsch, the regional coordinator for the National Rural Schools and Community Trust (formerly the Annenberg Rural Challenge). Julie has been instrumental in connecting us to similar work being done in schools around the country. The Vermont Rural Partnership, which grew out of an Annenberg grant, has also been a timely catalyst for fostering school-community partnerships by cultivating a place-based pedagogy dedicated to sustaining rural culture.

Meanwhile, schools and school districts in different parts of the country, many of them featured in this manual, deserve recognition for their pathbreaking work connecting students to the history of their own community. The Northern California Rural Challenge Network under Mitch Mendosa has been a leader in facilitating student-led projects documenting oral histories in Anderson Valley. Michael Umphrey, the director of the Montana Heritage Project, has likewise been a great inspiration in the movement for curriculum focusing on local history and heritage. And among the most exemplary systemic initiatives is the Alaska Native Knowledge Network, including Native elders such as Esther Ilutsik, who along with so many of her colleagues are working in and out of classrooms and schools to fundamentally change the way instruction happens and knowledge is passed down. You are our true mentors!

Our Food Works staff has continued to be a wellspring of creativity and inspiration, especially the venerable Hope Emerson, a teacher, storyteller, mycologist, and wild edible aficionado. Laura Dintino, our sparkling guidebook coordinator and office manager, has also been an invaluable asset to this project.

Additionally, we extend our deep thanks to the Food Works Board of Directors, beginning with Dr. Eleanor Ott, whose commitment to reclaiming indigenous ways of knowing through storytelling and oral histories has motivated all our efforts to bring this guidebook to fruition. The guidance of board members Jim Higgins, Scott Cameron, Cindy Senning, Cathy Lerner, and Artemis Joukowsky has also been instrumental to our work.

For the publication of the Common Roots Guidebook Series, we are forever grateful to the entire Tipper family: Mima, Charlie, Jack, Willie, and Marley. As their family grows, so grows their commitment to strengthening the bonds between the generations.

As designer, layout person, publications liaison, and editor-in-chief, Kate Mueller has done an outstanding job in making this book come to life. Without her imagination and flexibility, none of this work would have seen the light of day. Deepest thanks also go to Mary Azarian for her beautiful artwork that graces so many of these pages; and to Bill Lynn for his initial layout and design efforts.

And we give our heartfelt appreciation to our families and loved ones, especially Sam and Sarah Skelding, Amy Goodman-Kiefer, Ethan Gilbert, Rachel Kemple, and Kelly Sullivan.

Finally, we remember with deepest thanks our ancestors who have walked this way before us and lived the connection between the spirit of the land and the consciousness of the people that we aspire to here today.

The greatest living examples of these ancestors, for us, have been our own fathers—Donald J. Kemple and the late Joseph F. Kiefer and Francis M. Skelding. You have lived this history, remembered the names and personalities and stories of our forebears, faithfully practiced the same humble traditions that you received from them, and passed those down to us as we in turn pass them down to future generations. We give our love and thanks to you and to all who have come before you.

Preface

Why Food Works

About Food Works and the Common Roots Press

As the global economy continues headlong into the information technology era, it has become clear that communities everywhere are facing a common but historically unprecedented challenge: to keep pace with the demands of free trade and global competition while maintaining their own unique identity and integrity—culturally and ecologically. The nagging question first posed at the end of World War II by a social historian from Africa seems more relevant today than ever: "How do we maintain our identity—preserve what is ours—and still achieve liberation or progress?"

Having now published several teacher's guides on place-based curriculum, our non-profit educational firm Food Works has shown that when people address this complex issue on a local level through their educational system—including schools, businesses, civic organizations, government, churches, and outreach programs—what results is a strong, self-motivated generation of young learners ready to take on the new challenges of a global society. Backed by their own community, this generation is practical and versatile enough to adapt to the changing demands of a high-tech world, and at the same time culturally aware and ecologically sensitive enough to be committed to maintaining the habitability of their own region.

This has been our program focus at Food Works since the inception in 1990 of our Common Roots Schools Program, a community-based curriculum development process for educators. Through our professional development courses, in-service workshops, instructional videos, and curriculum guidebook series, teachers are developing integrated learning units that focus on students' basic needs and primary interests in their immediate environment. This work is helping to broaden the educational agendas of communities around Vermont and across the country to include an ongoing process for understanding the natural and cultural heritage unique to every place; an understanding that serves as the common touchstone for each child's lifelong learning.

I just feel that there's this power now with the kids. They want to provide something, to give something back to the community. And if we can instill that want in them now, then they'll be able to fulfill what's expected of them when they're older; to be part of the community, to be responsible.

—Lynn Hervey, Grade 2–3 teacher and curriculum coordinator of Peacham School's Cultural Literacy Program

This process involves far more than schools and children. It includes elders sharing their stories and practical wisdom and local historians, naturalists, farmers, artisans, and other professionals who have maintained their connection to the experiences and lessons of our ancestors; plus homemakers, parents, families, and singles who understand the importance of cultivating a community of scholars committed to conserving and regenerating their sense of place. In short, locally focused curricula give schools a stake in their communities and give communities a stake in their schools.

Our mission at Food Works is to deepen the collective understanding of our immediate social and natural world by providing a learning environment that extends beyond the four walls of the classroom, the traditional limitations of the standard subject areas, and the socially prescribed boundaries between young and old, professional and amateur, expert and novice. Our integrated garden program (hence our name) is just one example of the approaches we use to accomplish this goal. Beginning with garden-based curricula then expanding to include all areas of a school's learning goals, children discover the connections between personal nutrition, local ecology, and natural history in the context of their own community's story as passed down by local elders. They can learn firsthand about the interrelations between their lives and the larger food, environmental, social, and economic issues of our time. And they can become competent, self-directed learners actively engaged in addressing real-life issues in their own communities.

In an emerging global society, the ultimate goals of all of us in education are virtually the same: to educate young and old alike to meet the economic, ecological, social, and cultural challenges wrought by an increasingly integrated, technologically oriented world. The question before us is whether to meet those challenges through the same subject-specific, grade-oriented, textbook-driven quantified curriculum of the nineteenth and twentieth centuries, or through an open-ended learning process that still emphasizes learning the fundamentals but in ways that speak to and reflect the experience and values of the learners themselves and the changing communities they live in.

We have already seen the effect of this first, results-oriented approach on once-thriving cultures, traditions and ecosystems across the globe, including here in North America. We now must ask if we can summon the collective will and resources to cultivate a more sustainable, earth-centered educational agenda that draws from those same natural and cultural traditions that are being so threatened by these increasingly untenable ways of thinking and learning.

Living Traditions is one small step down the path that says we can, and we must.

Foreword

COMMUNITY-BASED SCHOOLS

Recovering America's Lost Legacy

by U.S. Senator Patrick Leahy

The Green Mountain State has strong agricultural ties, and for generations we Vermonters have cherished the land, creating a rich agrarian history steeped in long-standing cultural and ecological traditions. From our earliest roots, Vermont residents have been deeply involved in promoting and enhancing rural life and in developing creative educational opportunities. One of Vermont's finest public servants, Justin Morrill, changed the face of agricultural education when he introduced a congressional resolution to create a national agriculture school. This resolution led to the Land-Grant College Act, which was signed into law by President Abraham Lincoln in 1862 and gave American colleges the initial resources needed to build agriculture and engineering schools. Vermont was one of the first three states to adopt the act. To date, more than twenty million individuals have graduated from land-grant colleges, benefitting from Justin Morrill's vision of providing a practical education to millions of Americans and enhancing civic life.

At the time the land-grant law was enacted, over 80 percent of the population lived in rural areas, and 60 percent earned their living by farming. Today, only 23 percent of Americans live in rural areas and less than 2 percent are farmers. During the same time period, the number of people who are fed by the food produced on each farm has increased from five to over one hundred forty. As our farms become fewer and fewer and the size of the individual number of farms diminishes, each generation becomes further removed from the traditions of their ancestors and less connected to the origins of their food.

John Dewey, a graduate of Vermont's only land-grant college and an advocate of education through experimentation and practical activity, once said that "it is through what we do in and with the world that we read its meaning and measure its value." We are now at a critical historic juncture, where education for all ages must increasingly include a real world connection that emphasizes an understanding of place and brings personal meaning to learning. Dewey went on to say:

> The difference that appears when occupations are made the articulating centers of school life is not easy to describe in words; it is a difference in motive, of spirit and atmosphere. As one enters a busy kitchen in which a group of children are actively engaged in the preparation of food, the psychological difference, the change from more or less passive and inert recipiency and restraint to one of buoyant outgoing energy, is so obvious as fairly to strike one in the face. Indeed, to those whose image of the school is rigidly set the change is sure to give a shock.

Vermont's educational experiences offer examples of how communities can take charge of their own schools to teach, not just the knowledge and skills needed to compete in the global economy, but a community ethic and sense of belonging that is so crucial for a complete education in a civil society. Vermont's experiences offer hope for maintaining our ties to the land, and to each other, and still have top quality schools and high-achieving students.

As we as a society become increasingly globalized, we as individuals tend to become more and more transient. The once simple question of where one is from has become increasingly complex due to the demands of work, education, and family. It is more important today than ever before to instill a sense of place into our youth, for with this sense of place comes a feeling of responsibility for one's own community.

For years, a Vermont education has often included service learning. This allows a student to form bonds with those whom they might never know if not for the opportunity created by volunteering. Service learning also encourages a student to delve into their community and to understand its roots.

It is in this spirit that Food Works has aptly grown—from an organization that directly assisted Vermont's neediest by working to alleviate hunger, to one that offers tools for educators and students to actively explore the roots of their community and its ecological and social history. This exploration not only instills appreciation and respect for community in our younger generation, it is an important step in reinvigorating both rural and urban America. While this guide serves primarily as a tool for teachers, it is also a call to action to the wider educational community, as well as the general public, for educating the next generation to honor and learn about our natural and cultural heritage and the living traditions that go along with it.

Contents

PART II *Through the Seasons: Local History Throughout the Year*

Introduction

CULTURAL LITERACY CURRICULA
Linking the Past to the Future

Cultural literacy is an intimate understanding of the literature, lore, common stories, traditional crafts and skills, religious beliefs, and folkways of our recent and distant past. *Living Traditions* is a cultural literacy curriculum guide designed to take teachers through a clear, step-by-step process for developing an integrated, standards-based curriculum that focuses on the stories, crafts, and agrarian traditions of their local community. As teachers develop their own place-based, interdisciplinary units, they draw from area resources, including libraries, museums, and historical societies, and the skills and experience of community members, such as elders, artisans, farmers, storytellers, parents, and others.

This guide has been designed to complement the documentary video, *Getting to Know You: Learning from the Wisdom of Our Elders*, developed collaboratively with the Peacham School in Peacham, Vermont. This first-of-its-kind educational video documents students learning from their elders the stories and traditions of their own community, an emergent curriculum that we hope will inspire other teachers.

It is common knowledge that perennial wisdom lives in the memories of our elders. We also know that, once heard, elders' stories remain deeply rooted in our children's minds. Increasingly, schools across America are discovering that elders hold the missing link that connects the time-bound lessons of our cultural heritage to the boundless promise of an ever-unfolding future. All that is wanting for most elders to share their stories is simply an invitation and some preparation. *Living Traditions* is that invitation and preparation.

What Are Living Traditions?

For centuries, America's diverse cultural heritage has been developed and passed down to succeeding generations through agrarian traditions: seasonal rituals and stories that teach essential lessons for sustaining a people in balance with the natural world. These teachings formed the foundation of a living curriculum, bringing to life the moral practices and concepts that have shaped the character of human and natural relationships.

Naturally, the culture of any society is unique to the environment and history that have shaped it. Everyone would agree, for example, that the ecologically rooted indigenous cultures of New England underwent dramatic change with the arrival of Europeans. Successive immigrant populations brought with them cultural traditions that reflected their own historical relationship with the land. So the stories of our communities are really the stories of the peoples who have come before—their relationships to one another and their relationship to the natural world around them.

Research into our cultural heritage uncovers the mysteries of how peoples in ages past understood themselves and their world. These traditional ways of knowing include everything from creation stories and religious ceremonies to the way people worked the land and cared for their children. Historically, preserving this link to the past has proven to be the cultural lifeline of agrarian societies, literally their means of survival.

Among both indigenous peoples and early European settlers, the carriers of these stories and traditions were elders who were treated with respect and dignity as the caretakers of time-honored knowledge and values essential to sustaining the community's livelihood. It was long understood that the role of elders was to pass on this legacy to children, and the younger generation's responsibility was to care for their elders. Typically, these traditional stories and ceremonies have conveyed critical information, such as: how, when, and where to grow food; which herbs have special medicinal values; where to find water; how to build shelter; and how to make sense of seemingly inexplicable natural events.

Through the centuries, indigenous cultures were able to maintain their continuity in large measure because they kept alive the traditions and myths of their ancestors and passed them down to their children. Invariably, these legends and customs have been rooted in the natural world, a testament to the power of earth-based stories and mythologies to both renew a culture season after season and maintain its stability over time.

Modern industrial culture, in contrast, seems to be in a state of flux, perpetually reinventing itself in step with the seemingly endless opportunities new technologies continually pose, the microchip being the most recent. As a result, contemporary communities have tended to lose day-to-day contact with the cultural lifeline of our ancestors, which once had been humankind's wellspring of sustenance and collective meaning. Now at the beginning of a new millennium, we are asking: Where is our cultural wellspring, and how can we recover it?

Why Living Traditions?

In modern times, the imperative for transmitting these essential teachings has been mostly lost as we have evolved to more highly technological ways of communicating and working, not tied to any specific place or social group. As a result, we have unconsciously severed the lifeline to our ancient memory of place, disconnecting ourselves from the tightly woven cultural fabric that had, in times gone by, intimately bound extended families and immediate communities. In short, we are becoming culturally illiterate.

The good news is we still have the opportunity to reweave this intricate tapestry of stories, legends, myths, and customs in contemporary school curricula. We are presently standing at a historic crossroads. We can continue to race headlong into a technological future and leave dormant our rich cultural history, which has shaped who we are today. Or, we can reclaim the cultural legacy that gives meaning to our relationship with our natural world to one another.

As a retired farmer once asked at an intergenerational luncheon at the Warren School in Warren, Vermont: "How can you know where you're going unless you know where you've come from?" How fitting that this gem of wisdom was passed on during a community meal!

Why Study Local History?

Becoming Culturally Literate

The conversation between children and elders has been broken. The elders have been forgotten, and they, in turn, are forgetting. Studying local history can bridge that gap by:

1. Reconnecting students to the age-old story of the land: its geology, ecology, and human history.
2. Building a sense of intimacy and purpose, which feeds children's curiosity about their home and community.
3. Providing a way of honoring elders and community members for their traditional knowledge, skills, and local folklore.
4. Providing a way to keep traditional knowledge alive for future generations.
5. Creating a living archive, a catalogue of local folklore.
6. Giving students an opportunity to learn first-hand from elders about how people have lived in this community over time.
7. Providing motivation and meaning to students in an array of subjects including history, science, language arts, and culture.
8. Making the abstract real, allowing students to touch and see history live and in action.
9. Allowing students to see how global-historical forces actually affect real-life communities and people.
10. Allowing students to see how their own communities affect and have affected the larger historical drama.
11. Encouraging us to understand history from the inside out, rather than the outside in.
12. Encouraging students to understand history and social studies on their own terms, rather than those of an expert.
13. Cultivating creative and imaginative thinking that goes beyond what textbooks alone are able to promote.
14. Developing integrative, holistic learners.

To Be of Use

Embedding Service-Learning

Two important outcomes that naturally result from implementing place-based cultural literacy programs are (1) service-learning and (2) reincorporating elders into mainstream community life. Elders are all too often ignored or forgotten in today's fast-paced economy. Consequently, elders are lonelier and more isolated than any other age group in our society. As students go out into the community to interview and collect stories from area seniors, invariably they are going to witness some of the suffering and genuine needs of the elderly. This may at first make students feel uncomfortable. However, once a relationship is established between the young and old, a natural empathy develops, fostering a desire within students to help, to be of use.

This empathy stimulates students to maintain ongoing relationships with the elders they have befriended. Some schools institute within their curriculum regular visits that involve giving gifts, singing songs, making crafts, delivering food, and sharing meals. Consequently, service gradually becomes the foundation of every local history project, and it is this give and take that reflects what education is truly all about—drawing out (Latin root, *educere*: to draw out).

Consistent with Food Works' founding philosophy, we have emphasized from the outset that to appreciate and understand Vermont's agrarian traditions we must first gain a deeper appreciation and understanding of the land, climate, flora, fauna, soil, waterways, and ecological history of this place we call home. In other words, being culturally literate requires us to also be ecologically literate. *Living Traditions* focuses on both.

Living Traditions:

The Power of Story- and Place-Based Curricula

Everyone has a story to tell. Every child, every parent, every landscape, and every community has its own unique story. Stories provide identity, define purpose, and give meaning to our lives.

History is, first and foremost, based on stories. Lessons from the past, wisdom shared by elders, and tales revealed through the study of environmental changes over time all re-create stories that serve as powerful tools for learning. Place-based curricula such as *Living Traditions* include each of these elements. Place-based curricula not only incorporate stories, they are, themselves, stories.

Perhaps the most important advantage of a living traditions curriculum is that it continually reinforces the importance of stories. Educators have long known that education—teaching and learning—involves both art and heart. Pedagogy is the art of teaching and stories are at the heart of learning. Stories exist in a variety of forms, such as written tales, storytelling, or lessons handed down from generation to generation. Regardless of form, all provide opportunities for learning.

The symbolism of story and school curricula goes even deeper. The two basic components of a local history curriculum—its various units of study and its comprehensive assessment plan—are also stories. Learning units are essentially stories. They flow in a logical sequence from beginning to end, engage and inform, and ultimately convey a message or messages. The ongoing nature of assessment qualifies it as a story as well for it tells a story of student progress.

As alluded to earlier, the term *place-based* refers to an interdisciplinary curriculum woven from threads of local cultural and natural heritage. A place-based curriculum is a local, living traditions curriculum that tells the story of a land and its people. It is a curriculum that utilizes a community's rich history and uniqueness to teach essential skills and concepts and stimulate discovery of the broader world.

Honoring and re-creating the traditions and folklore of the past, as it turns out, is a sound and practical way to educate our children. These fundamental teachings are the crux of whole-child development, for they provide the most holistic and personally relevant experience possible—a foundation from which children will eagerly begin constructing knowledge and ultimately creating their own future.

In addition to helping cultivate a sense of place, a curriculum based on living traditions also provides real-world experiences for students. With its focus on natural (environment) and cultural (community) heritage, this curriculum naturally leads to learning beyond the classroom. The schoolyard and local community become laboratories—microcosms of the larger world students will go on to discover. Exploring the world outside the classroom not only enhances real-world connections for students, but it also provides the alternative learning environments and learning opportunities they need to succeed.

Both the content (local natural and cultural heritage) and context (school-community-environment) of a living traditions curriculum are relevant to every child's experience. The curriculum is personally meaningful and highly engaging. It is also inherently developmentally appropriate. It begins with a focus on local content, then builds to a developmentally more advanced holistic view of the world.

Curriculum activities focused locally also allow for multiple learning opportunities to occur, such as hands-on experiences, cooperative group work, collaboration, problem-solving, accommodating different intelligences and learning styles, and the creation of interdisciplinary curricula.

Some argue that this turning inward—into ourselves, into our communities, and into nature—will not help students meet the demands of globalized, standards-based education. But growing numbers of teachers, parents, and community members now recognize that place-based instruction complements what we know is essential to the learning process: connections, context, and continuity. Honoring and re-creating the traditions and folklore of the past, as it turns out, is a sound and practical way to educate our children. These fundamental teachings are the crux of whole-child development, for they provide the most holistic and personally relevant experience possible—a foundation from which children will eagerly begin constructing knowledge and ultimately creating their own future.

How to Use This Manual

Living Traditions is a blueprint for developing sustainable, local history curricula through the grades. Part I presents a systematic, eight-step process for developing and implementing a schoolwide cultural literacy curriculum focused on the history and cultural heritage of the local community. Step 1 describes a comprehensive ten-stage process for creating and implementing local, standards-based cultural literacy units. Although this section can stand alone as an effective tool for developing place-based curricula, we have found that when this process is undertaken as part of the larger program that continues with Steps 2 to 8, an authentic, sustainable, community-based program results. Students, teachers, elders, and other community members all collaborate in a true school-community partnership. It is this ideal that prompts us to encourage teachers to utilize all eight steps when developing their local history/cultural heritage units.

Part II has a complete sample unit for the fall season and an outline for a possible winter unit. Interspersed throughout the guide are activities that teachers from around Vermont have used to teach local history both in and out of the classroom, plus a wealth of resources for guiding students to research and discover the rich heritage of their neighborhood, town, and region.

How individual teachers or schools implement these activities, projects, and units of study will, however, be as unique to their own circumstances and aspirations as their community's history is distinct from that of their neighboring towns and villages. In short, there is, by definition, no textbook method for undertaking a local history curriculum.

This Living Traditions *curriculum guide is designed specifically to help teachers meet the highest educational standards by drawing on the unique cultural resources of their immediate community.*

Therefore, we encourage every teacher to take the path that seems right for his or her students' interests and academic goals. Start where it seems most natural and convenient, and allow the process to unfold on its own. You can begin with an elder who has deep family roots in the community and can share stories and practical skills with students; an archive or artifact that can form the center of an inquiry; a local event that is commemorated annually; or a newspaper article or story that might spark students' interest and motivate them to find out more.

Although *Living Traditions* contains dozens of such starting points, the aim of this book is to encourage teachers and administrators to systematically develop their own comprehensive, grade-by-grade local history curricula. Before following the eight-step method outlined in this book, we suggest first watching the video *Getting to Know You: Learning from the Wisdom of Our Elders*, the educational documentary the book is based on. This documentary illustrates the eight-step process for developing a schoolwide local history program, described in detail in Part I. After watching *Getting to Know You*, we suggest using the checklist on page 178 to brainstorm a preliminary list of topics and themes, local resource people, and project ideas for your own program.

A Word About Standards

Nationally, educational standards have affected virtually every aspect of our public school system from teaching and assessment to public policy and accountability. Educators are now faced with the daunting challenge of aligning their curricula to state and national standards while still maintaining control over the methodology and content taught in their own classrooms.

Increasingly, educators are discovering that what is at stake is nothing less than keeping intact the strong American tradition of local control over our children's education, not to mention sustaining the unique cultural heritage of America's communities. In the current educational climate, only when lesson plans and activities are aligned with standards will teachers be able to implement their own locally focused curricula that allows students to become culturally literate citizens in their community. This *Living Traditions* curriculum guide is designed specifically to help teachers meet the highest educational standards by drawing on the unique cultural resources of their immediate community.

One purpose of *Living Traditions* is to demonstrate how both standards and the distinctive character of every community can be addressed in a complementary way. The local history curriculum development process outlined here and the sample units and activities provided are all aligned to the Vermont Standards, showing how state standards naturally fit within the context of local customs and traditions.

Through our work with teachers over the past decade, we have found that the best way to motivate students to achieve the highest academic standards is by providing curricula relevant to the needs of the students in the context of their own community. In other words, for a curriculum to be engaging it must be culturally responsive and place-based.

We hope that *Living Traditions* is a lasting contribution to this growing movement—and ancient tradition—of place-based curricula toward which so many schools and communities are now returning.

Sample K–6 Local History Framework

Grade	Integrated Focus Question	Map	Social Studies Theme	Oral History Project	Sample Investigation Topics
K	What was the childhood of elders in my community like?	A family tree in pictures	Self	Elder storytelling	Elders sharing their childhood diaries with children
1	How has family life in my community changed over time? Stayed the same?	Home maps	Home (family)	Big books of elders	Family histories, family trees; diet, foods; recreation; work; travel
2	Who lived in my neighborhood? How has it changed? What did it look like before it was a neighborhood?	Neighborhood map	Neighborhoods	House-to-house neighborhood interviews	Architecture: When were these houses built? By whom? Why? School: What is the history of my school?
3	What is special about my community? Who were the first settlers here? Where did they come from? What happened to them?	Community maps	Community	Skit, musical, mural, photo essay, or display	Indigenous peoples: crafts, foods, shelter, ceremonies, travel
4	What were the cultural traditions of my region? What are the natural features of my watershed?	State and regional maps	State, region	Interview Native American elders	Regional folklore, indigenous culture
5	How does our community reflect the cultural traditions of the United States? What contribution has our community made to U.S. history?	U.S. geographical and topographical maps	U.S. history	Interview elders on how national holidays were once celebrated	Cultural traditions, ceremonies, and rituals unique to our community
6	What cultures from around the world have influenced our community and in what ways? What is the role of our community in world history?	Globe	World history	Interview immigrants to your community, old and new	Ethnic traditions and foods from around the world in our community

Eight Steps for Developing a Cultural Literacy Program in Your Community

1. Plan a standards-based curriculum.
2. Identify a community coordinator.
3. Prepare students.
4. Prepare the community participants (elders, etc.).
5. Community members teach/share with students.
6. Students give back to the community.
7. Culminating celebration.
8. Assessment and reflection.

Part I

Eight-Step Process for Developing a Comprehensive Local History Program

Step 1

Planning the Local History Curriculum

To begin planning a standards-based unit in local history, teachers are best served by undergoing a basic orientation to the community in which their students live. This orientation process begins with researching and understanding the natural history of the land and how it has shaped human settlements over time. Teachers gain this understanding through local natural and cultural heritage mapping. The mapping process is followed by a rigorous inventory of the needs and assets of the community to create a general profile of the students, families, school, and wider community. The information obtained during these first two steps then frames the local story from which specific focus areas of student inquiry can be determined.

Once the focus areas of the local story have been defined, the design of the local history unit itself begins by first identifying the state and district standards that will be addressed throughout the unit. The enabling activities that are created as a result are intentionally designed as building blocks to help students learn the story of their community while attaining the identified standards. These assessment activities lead to a culminating community event that provides a rich opportunity for performance-based assessment as students share their work with parents and community members.

Ten Stages for Designing a Local Standards-Based Unit

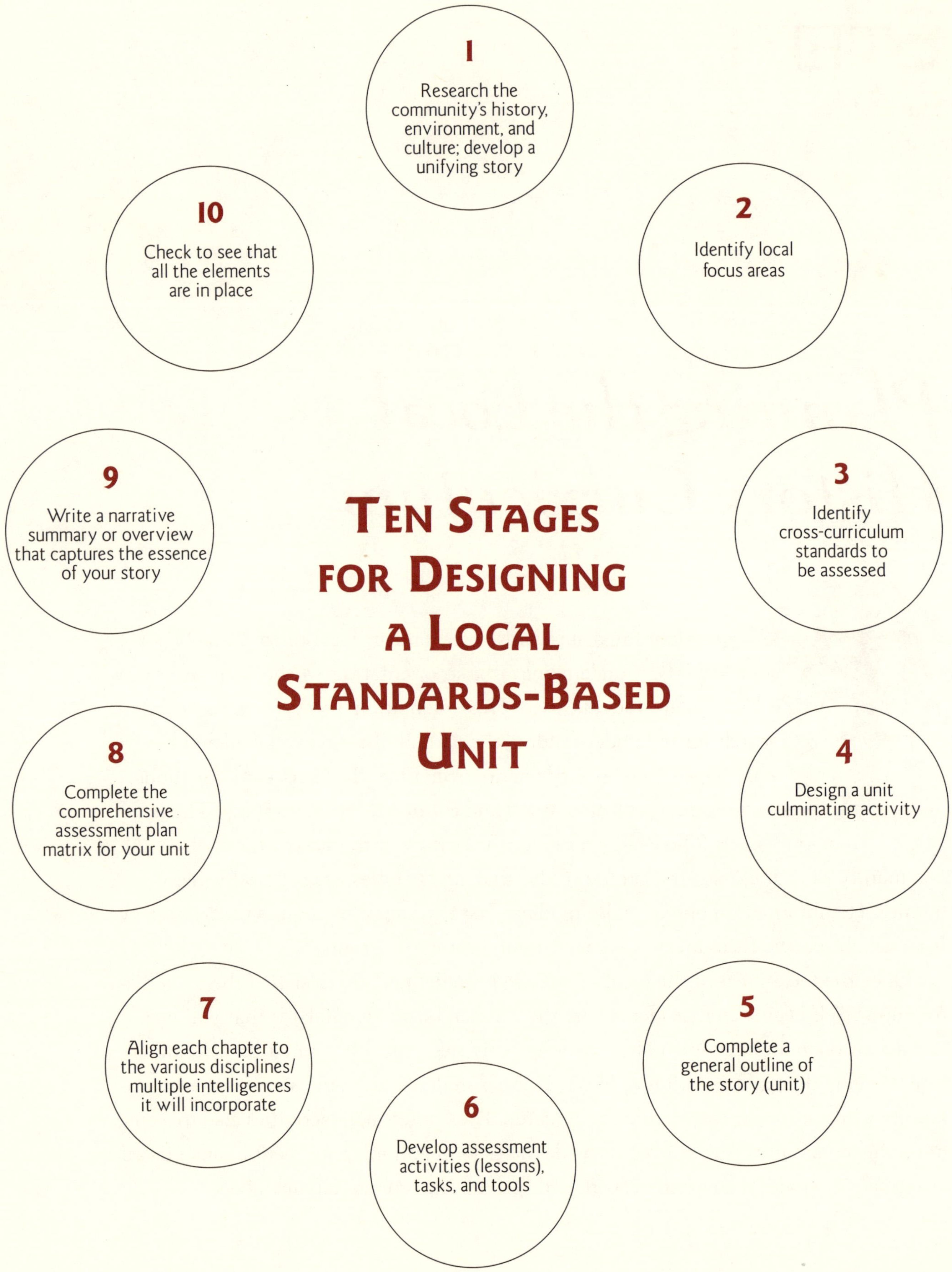

1
Research the community's history, environment, and culture; develop a unifying story

2
Identify local focus areas

3
Identify cross-curriculum standards to be assessed

4
Design a unit culminating activity

5
Complete a general outline of the story (unit)

6
Develop assessment activities (lessons), tasks, and tools

7
Align each chapter to the various disciplines/multiple intelligences it will incorporate

8
Complete the comprehensive assessment plan matrix for your unit

9
Write a narrative summary or overview that captures the essence of your story

10
Check to see that all the elements are in place

An Overview of the Ten Stages

Stage 1

Research your community's environment, history, and present-day culture through natural history mapping, cultural heritage mapping, and community profiling. (See "Natural History Inquiry," page 23, and "Cultural Heritage Inquiry," page 24, and the community, school, and student profiles on pages 25 to 27.)

Stage 2

Identify local history and cultural foci that tell the unique story of your community and address the needs and assets identified in the profiles you created in Stage 1.

Stage 3

Identify cross-curricula standards to be assessed that naturally align with the local story you plan to re-create. (See page 29 for an example of an embedded-standards list.)

Stage 4

Design a "Grand Culminating Activity" that will celebrate your story's message and provide students the opportunity to demonstrate their attainment of the standards your unit addresses. (See Form A, "Grand Culminating Activity," page 31.)

Stage 5

Complete a general outline of your story (unit) that sequentially lists the "chapters" (basic concepts and topics) you plan to cover. (See Form B, "General Outline," page 32.)

Stage 6

Develop assessment activities (lessons), tasks, and tools that align with your chapters and the standards your unit addresses. (See Form C, "Activity/Lesson Plans," page 33, and your embedded standards list.) Keep in mind Learning Opportunities Standards such as multiple intelligences, cooperative learning, and gender equity when designing your activities.

Stage 7

Align each chapter to the various disciplines they incorporate, as well as the multiple intelligences they address. (See Form D, "Multiple Intelligences Web," and Form E, "Interdisciplinary Web," on pages 35 to 37.)

Stage 8

Complete Form F, "Classroom Comprehensive Assessment Plan Matrix" (page 38), paying special attention to the generalized-standard assessment that will occur during your unit.

Stage 9

Write a narrative summary that captures the flow of your story (unit) and a rationale for why this story is worth re-creating and exploring. (See Form G, "Summary/Rationale," page 39.)

Stage 10

Check to see that all the elements of your standards-based, local community unit are in place. (See Form H, "Standards-Based Unit Checklist," page 40.)

Stage 1
Local Research

Why Research?

In the modern classroom, it is common for students to engage in projects that are meaningful and interesting in themselves, but have relatively little connection to one another or to the natural and cultural environment with which students are most familiar. As a result, students often fail to see any inherent connection or greater purpose to their studies from season to season or from grade to grade, nor do most children readily see how their academic work relates to their life at home or in the community.

More and more teachers are finding, however, that when they take up an active interest in the life and history of the community that their students live in, it deepens their understanding of the forces that have shaped who their students are and allows them to develop a more personally relevant curriculum for their students.

Undertaking the task of conducting background research into the community that they teach in—including the environment, the history, the demographics, and the needs and assets of their students—provides teachers with a rich foundation to build meaningful, authentic curricula relevant to their students' needs and everyday interests. From this background research, teachers can begin a schoolwide visioning and strategic planning process to reinvent a local, grade-by-grade, near-to-far curriculum that reflects the history and ecology of their students' community.

Background Research Questions

The following guided inquiry process is designed as a curriculum development activity for teachers to gather background information on the history, culture, demographics, and ecology of the wider community. This research informs teachers of the opportunities for practical, applied learning that will benefit not only the students but the greater community. Students, as well, can participate in Stage 1. Teachers might choose to have students participate throughout the process or during select portions of the process.

Teachers begin by using the following five questions to determine the local story that their students will research and re-create as a unit of study. These questions first and foremost help reorient teachers to the resources available beyond their classrooms. They rediscover the ways in which the community can be a learning environment larger and more promising than the classroom alone. This exploration will provide the information teachers need to create a place-based curricula.

1. Where are we? (Natural Heritage Mapping)
Using maps and natural heritage inquiries (see "Natural History Inquiry," page 23), teachers first become familiar with the geography, geology, and natural history of the area. Typically at this early stage, teachers invite an area historian from the historical society, along with elders who can tell stories about local history and changes in the land they've witnessed over time. Local geologists and natural historians might also be invited to share their expertise.

2. Who were we? (Cultural Heritage Mapping)
Teachers follow up by conducting a cultural heritage inquiry, investigating the history of the community (see "Cultural Heritage Inquiry," page 24). They begin by visiting an area library or historical society to learn more about the chronological and cultural history of the people who settled in the community. Typically, teachers will create a historical timeline to use as a reference for later place-based projects.

3. Who are we today?
(Needs and Assets Inventory)
Demographic assessments and school and community profiles provide teachers with valuable information on the present-day culture and cultural trends of their village, town, or city, as well as the specific needs of their students and community (see community, school, and student profiles, pages 25 to 27). This stage can culminate in a wide-ranging discussion of

Sharing stories and essential information on basic living skills between the generations was once taken for granted as a natural part of children's education in their community. Intergenerational learning has only been dropped from the modern school curriculum in the past five to six decades and is now experiencing a revival in many forward-thinking school districts and classrooms.

the broader implications of this profile for teaching and learning (see "Community, School, and Student Profiles: Implications and Next Steps," page 28). For example, if 40 percent of the children in school are on free or reduced lunches, what should the teachers be teaching these children? How do they respond to their students' immediate and longer term needs?

4. What will be our future?
(Visioning and Strategic Planning)

During this step teachers develop a vision statement describing specific plans for local history research, documentation, presentation, and long-term curriculum integration. This is an ideal time for teachers to begin developing a long-term relationship with their local historical society and senior centers. Teachers, at this point in the process, are now striving to intentionally develop not just a one-shot project but a curricular foundation to their evolving school culture. The following questions can help this visioning and strategic planning process:

- How do we pass on to future generations a deep appreciation for local history? How can we make our school a repository for local archives, artifacts, and primary sources (such as photographs and diaries) to be used by teachers and students as part of an ongoing local history curriculum and by community members to further their appreciation for their community's heritage?
- Systematically, how do we go about doing this schoolwide so that every grade plays a part in collecting, remembering, and honoring our local history? What skills, knowledge, activities, and methods do we as teachers need to prepare us to teach about the community's local history?
- How do we show our appreciation to elders for their wisdom? How can we give back to them through service-learning projects (gifts, food, visits, helping with chores)? How do we embed service-learning into all our local history work so that students learn the give and take that is our common language?

5. What is the unifying story of our community?
(Curriculum Mapping)

With the information gathered from answering these initial questions combined with the developmental needs and interests of the students, teachers can then weave the overall story of the community. This story, in effect, is a synthesis of the answers to the questions posed in the first four steps. What ecosystem evolved from these geologic formations? What peoples first settled here and how did they live? Who came later and why? The story then follows the settlement patterns of community ancestors. Finally, the story explores the present-day community, the ways in which it reflects those who shaped and framed the community through the generations, and concludes by addressing the present-day needs and assets of the community.

This is the overriding story we need to find our way through a developmentally appropriate school-wide curriculum. It is the guiding context for the development of any curriculum of place.

Stage 2
Local History Focus Areas

Drawing from the research conducted and unifying story developed during Stage 1, teachers then choose an era, event, or topic that will serve as the theme for their local history unit. This local history theme, or focus area, can be built around virtually any person, place, issue, or landmark that the students might be interested in investigating.

A second grade class, for example, may decide to focus on the origins and names of the first families that settled in the community. The teacher can then use the cultural heritage maps the students developed during Stage 1 to review the settlement patterns and first families of the neighborhoods they choose. This focus area might be called "Discovering the First Families of Our Neighborhoods."

Stage 3
Standards Alignment

Once general focus areas are determined, teachers then identify the learning standards they need or want to address at their grade level and that align to the local history focus areas they and their students are investigating (see "Embedded Standards: A Sample List," page 29, for a list of some of Vermont's standards that align to local history content). This step is critical because to proceed in developing specific content and activities, teachers must first be familiar with the standards and criteria that content and those activities must ultimately address and allow for assessment of student progress.

Stage 4
Culminating Activity

At this stage, teachers look ahead to determine an appropriate community event through which students can demonstrate their mastery of the content, skills, and standards addressed throughout the local history unit. This culminating activity might include demonstrations, presentations, performances, exhibits, and/or displays (see Form A, "Grand Culminating Activity," page 31).

The second grade unit mentioned above could culminate with student-made relief maps, a big book of photos and interviews of neighborhood elders, and reenactments of songs, games, and dances popular in the neighborhood in years gone by. All these activities would be presented by the students not only to share their learning with parents and community members, but to demonstrate their progress toward attaining the academic standards addressed through a context of local history, beginning with the neighborhoods in which they live.

Stage 5
General Outline

After the culminating activity is determined, teachers then decide what steps to take to prepare students for this event. Teachers first determine a sequence of general concepts or topics that will serve as building blocks for the overall unit and create multiple opportunities to address the standards being assessed. These topics, in essence, are the "chapters" to the overall story being re-created (see Form B, "General Outline," page 32).

Chapters for the second grade neighborhood unit might include: (1) "Where Are We on the Map," (2) "My House Is Different Than Yours," (3) "What Life Was Like Growing Up in Our Neighborhood," (4) "What Life Is Like for Us Growing Up Here," (5) "Traditions in Our Neighborhood," and (6) "Nature in Our Neighborhood."

It is crucial when deciding what chapters to plan to root each one in the local environment and the culture that has been shaped by that environment, as well as ensure that each aligns to the embedded standards that are helping shape the unit.

STAGE 6
Assessment Activities (Lessons), Tasks, and Tools

This stage is the heart of the unit for it details the specific lessons (content/activities) and the accompanying assessment tasks and tools (scoring guides) teachers plan to incorporate into their local history focus (see Form C, "Activity/Lesson Plan," page 33). The assessment component is critical because it informs instruction, provides feedback to students and teachers, and helps ensure that students are provided multiple opportunities to attain the standards being assessed.

One assessment activity for the second grade neighborhood unit (Chapter 3: "What Life Was Like Growing Up in Our Neighborhood") might be to have students interview local elders. Teachers might start by conducting a knowledge preassessment of their students to determine what they already know about life in the past. This preassessment might consist of a simple task such as a concept web on which students are asked to list what they know related to a topic, such as "Life in the Old Days." Teachers might also choose to include at this time a preassessment of where students stand in relation to the criteria of some of the standards being addressed and assessed through this unit. For example, two of Vermont's standards that naturally align with this activity/unit are 1.13 Listening and 6.6 Being a Historian. Based on their knowledge of their students' abilities prior to this unit, teachers simply fill in for each student a generalized-standard checklist or rubric for these particular standards (see Appendix B). For a more complete picture of where students are in relation to these standards and their criteria, have the students self-assess using these checklists and rubrics as well.

These preassessments inform the students of what they know and don't know and where they stand in terms of attaining the standards. They also inform teachers of students' prior knowledge and pre- and misconceptions, which in turn helps direct instruction. In addition, these preassessments inform students about what they will be investigating, the skills they will be working on, and levels of performance expected of them.

Once preassessments are completed, teachers are ready to engage their students in the assessment activities themselves. In this particular activity—interviewing elders—students will not only have the chance to acquire more knowledge about the topic they're investigating (i.e., "What Life Was Like Growing Up in Our Neighborhood"), they will also have the opportunity to progress toward attaining the standards involved (i.e., Listening and Being a Historian). The actual performances of the students and the products they generate during this activity will serve as additional means to help assess their knowledge acquisition and progress in the standards.

On completing the assessment activity, teachers will then conduct a postassessment to determine what progress was made and where to go next. For an obvious comparison of before and after, teachers might choose to use the same tasks and tools (scoring guides) used during the preassessment.

STAGE 7
Interdisciplinary Connections and Multiple Intelligences

Once teachers determine their assessment activities, tasks, and tools, their next step is to ensure these activities provide interdisciplinary connections and address the multiple intelligences. Using Form E, "Interdisciplinary Web" (page 38), teachers can map their planned activities and view the distribution of these activities in the disciplines being incorporated. This process enables teachers to be proactive in explaining to parents and school board members the interdisciplinary value of studying local history. Though certain factors may prohibit every discipline from being incorporated, a balance can be struck in creating a rich, well-rounded unit.

During this stage, teachers also map their activities with the multiple intelligences, assessing whether or not a balance of opportunities exists for students with varying learning styles (see Form D, "Multiple Intelligences Web," page 35). Below is a list of activities for each of the eight multiple intelligences that could be incorporated into the second grade neighborhood unit described earlier.

Logical/Mathematical	Creating neighborhood timelines
Linguistic	Composing poems describing their neighborhoods
Musical	Learning songs of yesteryear
Bodily/Kinesthetic	Playing games of yesteryear
Visual/Spatial	Creating neighborhood maps
Interpersonal	Interviewing neighborhood elders
Intrapersonal	Maintaining personal journals
Naturalist	Sensory explorations of neighborhood habitats
Existentialist	Tracing community culture back to its believed origin

STAGE 8
Classroom Comprehensive Assessment Plans

Using the "Classroom Comprehensive Assessment Plan Matrix" (see Form F, page 38), teachers document the standards their activities (or unit) address and how frequently those standards are addressed and student performance assessed. In addition, teachers keep track of the means by which student performance in those standards is being assessed to ensure their assessment plan is multifaceted. Again, this is critical because students have different learning styles. For example, a linguistic-oriented student will be able to effectively express what he or she knows through written products, whereas an interpersonal-oriented student might fare better through performances or conferences.

The matrix serves as a way for teachers to map their assessment-based instruction. The completed matrix will show any gaps in the overall assessment plan, allowing the teacher to return to the unit chapters/activities and include more diverse assessment activities, tasks, and tools. For example, if teachers find that their plans incorporate many more tools (rubrics and checklists) than products, they can then go back and build in more opportunities for their students to create products that will also demonstrate what they know and are able to do.

STAGE 9
Narrative Summary and Rationale

In this stage, teachers write a one-page overview—a short story—of what the unit is about and why it is worth re-creating with students (see Form G, "Summary and Rationale," page 39). It is important that teachers anchor the narrative in the history, environment, and culture of their community, explaining how this focus area fits the unifying story developed in Stage 1, and how this story meets the developmental needs of the students.

Who says school's not fun? Girls dance in the mud to soften the clay skin for their Quebec-style outdoor bread oven.

A narrative for the second grade unit, "Discovering the First Families of Our Neighborhoods," might first explain why this focus area was chosen for second grade students. Next, it would briefly describe the history of the land and the people who have settled there. It might also generally describe some of the activities and investigations that will take place, including the culminating activity.

STAGE 10
Unit Assessment

Teachers conclude the first cycle of the process by reviewing Form H, "Standards-Based Unit Checklist" (page 40). This form provides teachers with a list of the criteria and components of standards-based units. It can be used to help guide the creation of standards-based units, as well as assess how well they meet the criteria required of standards-based units. If this checklist reveals that there are missing pieces in the planned unit, teachers can then go back and ensure that a more comprehensive unit is in place and ready to implement.

What follows is an example of a local, standards-based unit developed by the Newport Town School in Newport Center, Vermont, using the ten stages outlined above.

Outdoor Bread Ovens of Newport

1–2. First conduct local research and identify the story and local cultural foci you and your class want to explore and retell. This story becomes the unit to be studied. The Newport Town School, for example, wanted to re-create the story of the Quebec-style bread ovens that were used by the early settlers of Vermont's Northeast Kingdom, so they first conducted research on bread ovens, which ultimately culminated with the building of their own bread oven during their Spring Unit, called "Outdoor Bread Ovens of Newport."

3. Once the story (and essential question[s]) and local cultural foci are identified, determine the standards that will be addressed and assessed during the unit. The Newport Town School unit addressed and assessed student performance in some of the embedded standards found on "Embedded Standards: A Sample List" (page 29).

4. The class then brainstorms a culminating activity that will allow students to demonstrate to the community the learning that took place during the unit (Form A, page 31). The Newport Town School concluded their unit by holding a community-wide ceremony and

Once they've softened the mud with their feet, the girls pack it onto the frame of the bread oven. (This activity is part of an integrated social studies/nutrition/design technology unit in local history at the Newport Town School in Vermont's Northeast Kingdom.)

bread-making festival using their outdoor bread oven, which included student presentations, demonstrations of how to use the oven, and bread recipes that they collected from friends and family.

5. Next, the story or unit is divided into several "chapters" or topics that individual students and teams can research (Form B, page 32). Topics Newport Town students explored included early French settlements, food grown in northern Vermont during the colonial period and the diet of the colonists, and settlement patterns in Vermont's Northeast Kingdom.

6.–7. Activities (lessons) for each of these "chapters" then need to be developed. These activities are designed to contribute toward the culminating activity and allow for ongoing assessment of student learning and progress toward attainment of the standards (Form C, page 33). The entire story should then be mapped out using an interdisciplinary web (Form E, page 37) and multiple intelligences web (Form D, page 37) to ensure the unit is accommodating best practices.

8. Once these activities and their accompanying assessments are identified, teachers then complete the Classroom Comprehensive Assessment Plan Matrix (Form F, page 38).

9. A narrative summary helps solidify for everyone what the unit is about and provides a rationale for why the unit is worth doing (Form G, page 39). Aside from providing students an opportunity to progress toward attaining particular standards, Newport Town School's rationale included the importance of exposing students to the rich agricultural heritage of their local community.

10. Finally, the "Standards-Based Unit Checklist" (Form H, page 40) is used to make sure that all the components and criteria for implementing a standards-based unit have been met.

Natural History Inquiry

What is the story of the land where our community now exists, and what are some of its unique qualities?

Focus Questions

1. What do we know about the geologic history of this land? What more do we want to find out?

2. Where is our community located and how does this location make our community unique?

3. What watershed is our community a part of and how has it changed over time?

4. What natural habitats have adapted to these landforms over time?

5. What impact has the ecology of this area had on the people who have lived here?

CULTURAL HERITAGE INQUIRY

What is the story of human settlement in our area, and how has it changed over time?

Focus Questions

1. What is the cultural history of this area beginning with indigenous peoples?

2. How has the culture of this area adapted to the local geography?

3. What are the different ethnic backgrounds of people who have settled here?

4. What are some unique cultural characteristics of this area?

5. How have local demographics changed over time?

6. What social and economic challenges do people living here today face and how have those challenges changed over time?

7. What environmental issues did early inhabitants of this area face, and what are the environmental issues faced by inhabitants today?

Community Profile

Demographics

Strengths

Assets

Challenges

School Profile

Demographics

Strengths

Assets

Challenges

Student Profile

Demographics

Strengths

Assets

Challenges

Community, School, and Student Profiles
Implications and Next Steps

After completing the profiles on the previous pages, please answer the following questions.

1. Now that we know more about the demographics, strengths, assets, and challenges of our community, school, and students, how can we as educators respond?

2. How might I utilize or incorporate this information in developing my integrated, place-based curricula?

3. How might my integrated local history unit impact our current community, school, and student profiles?

Embedded Standards
A Sample List

Below is an example of an initial list of embedded standards for local, place-based curricula. Embedded standards are those inherent in any given content or context. Standards that are embedded in a given content area are naturally addressed and, therefore, readily assessed through that content.

1.18 INFORMATION TECHNOLOGY
Students use computers, telecommunications, and other tools of technology to research, gather information and ideas, and represent information and ideas accurately and appropriately.

1.19 RESEARCH
Students use organizational systems to obtain information from various sources (including libraries and the Internet).

2.2 PROBLEM SOLVING
Students use reasoning strategies, knowledge, and common sense to solve complex problems related to all fields of knowledge.

3.9 SUSTAINABILITY
Students make decisions that reflect understanding of ecosystems and the relationships (ecological, economic, political, social) within them and an awareness that their personal and collective actions affect the sustainability of these interrelated systems.

3.10 TEAMWORK
Students perform effectively on teams that set and achieve goals, conduct investigations, solve problems, and create solutions (e.g., by using consensus-building and cooperation to work toward group decisions).

4.1 SERVICE
Students take an active role in their community.

4.5 CONTINUITY AND CHANGE
Students understand continuity and change.

4.6 UNDERSTANDING PLACE
Students demonstrate understanding of the relationship between their local environment and community heritage and how each shapes their lives.

6.6 BEING A HISTORIAN
Students use historical methodology to make interpretations concerning history, change, and continuity.

6.8 MOVEMENTS AND SETTLEMENTS
Students analyze the factors and implications associated with the historical and contemporary movements and settlements of people in various times in their local community, in Vermont, in the United States, and in various locations worldwide.

7.1 SCIENTIFIC METHOD
Students use scientific methods to describe, investigate, and explain phenomena (raise questions, hypothesize, test, deduce, collect and analyze data, generate conclusions).

7.2 INVESTIGATION
Students design and conduct a variety of their own investigations and projects (questions, procedures, data collection and recording, data representation, conclusions).

7.7 GEOMETRIC AND MEASUREMENT CONCEPTS
Students use geometric and measurement concepts.

7.11 SYSTEMS: ANALYSIS
Students analyze and understand living and nonliving systems (e.g., biological, chemical, electrical, mechanical, optical) as collections of interrelated parts and interconnected systems.

7.13 ORGANISMS, EVOLUTION, AND INTERDEPENDENCE
Students understand the characteristics of organisms, see patterns of similarities and differences among living organisms, understand the role of evolution, and recognize the interdependence of all systems that support life.

Unit Development Form A
Grand Culminating Activity

Title ______________________________

Description

Include in your description an explanation of how the different components of this community-based activity incorporate your community story, local history focus area, and the various standards addressed throughout your local history unit.

Unit Development Form B
General Outline

Local History Focus Area ______________________________

Unit chapters (topics/concepts being covered)

I.

II.

III.

IV.

V.

VI.

VII.

VIII.

Unit Development Form C
ACTIVITY/LESSON PLAN

Title of Activity

Standard(s) Being Addressed

Inquiry/Focusing Questions

Topic

Materials

Procedures

Task-Specific Assessment

(products, performances, tasks, tools [rubrics/checklists], anecdotal observations)

Generalized-Standard Assessment

Unit Development Form D
MULTIPLE INTELLIGENCES WEB

Interpersonal

Intrapersonal

Bodily Kinesthetic

Naturalist

Unit (Story)

Musical

Visual/Spatial

Logical-Mathematical

Linguistic

Existentialist

Unit Development Form E
Interdisciplinary Web

Fine Arts

Community/Service

Science

Language Arts

Unit (Story)

Math

Social Studies

Technology

Unit Development Form E
Interdisciplinary Web (*Sample*)

Fine Arts

Food murals
Food collages
Culinary arts
Field songs and dances
Pumpkin carving gourds
Recipe book illustrating

Community/Service

Service learning
Local food policy
Emergency food shelf
Changing the role of food: from sacred to commercial

Science

Native wild foods
Ethnobotanicals
Local horticulture/gardening over time
Seed saving
Nutrition

What is the role of food in our local history?

Language Arts

Interviewing elders
Primary research
Diaries
Written reports on local food growing
Journaling ("A Day in the Life")

Math

Food economics
TImelines of settlement patterns
Local food-growing projections
Square foot measurements for a home food system

Social Studies

Diet of early settlers
Food-growing techniques
Hunger and food scarcity
Local food industry over time
Heirloom varieties

Technology

Food preservation techniques
Transportation of food
Cooking and baking techniques
Food growing: crop rotation
Bioengineering

Unit Development Form F

Classroom Comprehensive Assessment Plan Matrix

It is important that comprehensive assessment plans be fair, valid, meaningful, and effective. One step toward ensuring this is to keep a record of the variety, balance, and frequency of assessments taking place during the course of the year. An assessment plan matrix is a tool that can help simplify this task. Note that the matrix below gives particular attention to how often generalized-standard assessment occurs.

Unit/Activity ______________________ **Grade** __________

Standards	Number of Times Addressed	Number of Times Assessed	Type of Generalized-Standard Assessment				
			Product	*Performance*	*Task*	*Scoring Guide*	*Anecdotal Observations*

Unit Development Form G
Summary and Rationale

Local History Focus Area ______________________________

Summary (the essence and flow of your unit)

Rationale (why this unit is worth exploring)

Unit Development Form H
Standards-Based Unit Checklist

Assessment activities are often collectively arranged to create a unit. For a unit of study to qualify as standards-based, certain criteria must be met. Below is a checklist that can serve as both a reminder of what makes up a standards-based unit, as well as a means for assessing a unit, particularly in relation to standards and assessment.

_______ **Story (Unit)**

- _______ Addresses local cultural heritage.
- _______ Addresses local natural heritage.
- _______ Helps develop the child's sense of place.

_______ **Essential Question**

- _______ Addresses the general concepts (big picture) of the unit.
- _______ Addresses personal (student) relevance.
- _______ Students' answers (pre- and postassessment) serve as a means to assess their acquisition of knowledge and progress toward attaining the standards being addressed.

_______ **Standards**

- _______ One or more Vital Results* are addressed.
- _______ One or more Fields of Knowledge* are addressed.
- _______ One or more Learning Opportunities* are addressed.
- _______ Knowledge and skill standards are both addressed.
- _______ Generalized criteria are clearly stated and explained prior to start of unit.

_______ **Goals/Rationale**

- _______ Standards being addressed are clearly stated in the goals.
- _______ Rationale states why unit is worth doing and includes reference to the standards being addressed.

---

*These sample standards categories are taken from the Vermont Framework of Standards and Learning Opportunities.

______ **Culminating Activity**

______ Provides students with an opportunity to comprehensively demonstrate the knowledge they've acquired and the progress they've made toward attaining the standards being addressed during the unit.

______ **Focusing Questions**

______ are intriguing and reflective, and students' answers (pre- and postassessment) will serve as a means to assess their acquisition of knowledge and progress toward attaining the standards being addressed.

______ **Enabling (Assessment) Activities**

______ are developmentally appropriate and align to the standards being addressed.

______ allow for simultaneous instruction and assessment of those standards being addressed.

______ provide multiple opportunities for students to work toward attaining the standards being addressed.

______ accommodate the multiple intelligences and incorporate interdisciplinary connections.

______ result in products and performances that authentically assess both acquisition and application of knowledge.

______ result in products and performances that authentically assess student progress in the standards being addressed.

______ **Comprehensive Assessment Plan**

______ aligns to the standards and criteria being addressed.

______ includes ongoing monitoring of student progress toward attainment of the standards being addressed.

______ includes a balance of assessment products, performances, tasks, scoring guides (tools), and anecdotal observations.

______ includes a balance of task-specific and generalized-standard assessment.

______ **Exemplars**

______ demonstrate unit's effectiveness in helping students attain the standards and acquire the knowledge being addressed.

SHOW ME THE WAY
Creating a 3-D Community Map

Standard(s) Being Addressed

1.18	Information Technology	6.6	Being a Historian
1.19	Research	6.8	Movements and Settlements
2.2	Problem Solving	7.11	Systems: Analysis
3.10	Teamwork		

Inquiry/Focusing Questions

If you were a bird, what would you see when you fly over your community?

How many buildings are in your community? How many people live there?

How far from your house does your community extend?

What does the landscape of your community look like from the air?

How is the surrounding landscape impacting your community?

How is your community impacting the surrounding landscape?

Why is there such a strong connection between the natural heritage and cultural heritage of a community?

Topic

Creating a three-dimensional map of our community that includes both its natural and cultural assets.

Materials

reference materials (e.g., state agency documents, local planning commission maps, Geographic Information Survey [GIS] maps, town maps, aerial photographs)

variety of art/construction media (papier-mâché, clay, tissue paper, Play-Doh, cardboard, construction paper, scissors, paint, brushes)

adequate-sized tables or sheets of plywood

adequate work and display space

graph paper

logs (composition booklets work well)

blank concept webs

Procedures

1. Preassess students individually using a concept web to find out what they know about their community.
2. Divide students into heterogeneous groups (encourage cooperative learning skills and division of labor).
3. Review with students the definition of community and the various natural (flora, fauna, terrain, water, soil, weather, climate) and cultural assets (structures, architecture, transportation, neighborhoods, downtown/business districts) that exist within a community.
4. Begin collecting data, starting with a survey of the school grounds and its surrounding landscape. Ask students to record in their logs general observations of local natural and cultural assets and map those assets on their graph paper. Remind students that they will ultimately be using the data they collect and the maps they draw to create three-dimensional panorama maps of their community.
5. Extend data collection to include the broader town/community by taking a field trip around town, recording additional natural and cultural assets.
6. Further identify the community's surrounding landscape and cultural assets by having students supplement their data collection using the references listed under Materials.
7. Ask students to synthesize the data collected in their logs, their graph paper maps, and their reference research and use that combined information to create three-dimensional maps that represent their community. (*Note:* Each group could create its own map, or each could create one section of a whole-class map.)
8. Engage students in a discussion on the activity's focusing questions.
9. Assess students' acquisition of knowledge and progress toward attaining the standards being addressed.

Task-Specific Assessment

(products, performances, tasks, tools [rubrics/checklists], anecdotal observations)

logs   graph paper maps   3-D maps   pre- and postconcept webs
anecdotal observations of teamwork and discussion times

Generalized-Standard Assessment

1.18 Information Technology checklist   3.10 Teamwork rubrics

THE WIZARD'S STAFF
Creating Your Own Special Ceremony

Standard(s) Being Addressed

1.18	Information Technology	3.10	Teamwork
1.19	Research	4.5	Continuity and Change
2.2	Problem Solving	6.6	Being a Historian

Inquiry/Focusing Questions

Why do people hold celebrations and conduct special ceremonies?

When and how did the ceremonies we practice get started?

If we were to create a ceremony that honored our community, what would that ceremony look like? What aspect(s) of our community would it honor?

How might we honor the way(s) our surrounding landscape impacts our community?

How might we honor the way(s) our community impacts our surrounding landscape?

Why is there such a strong connection between the natural heritage and cultural heritage of a community?

Topic

Creating a ceremony to honor the natural and cultural assets of our community.

Materials

reference materials relating to the subject of choice being honored

variety of art/construction media for costumes (papier-mâché, tissue paper, clay, Play-Doh, cardboard, construction paper, scissors, paint, brushes)

ingredients and required cooking utensils for preparation of ceremonial foods

already prepared food, music and/or costumes for cases where time does not allow for the students to create their own

musical instruments

video recorder

blank KWL forms (See form in Appendix B, page 180; KWL defined on page 66.)

Procedures

1. Schedule a time for students to present their ceremonies and begin advertising (posters, fliers, notices by mail) and inviting the community to attend this special event.
2. Preassess students individually using a KWL graphic organizer to find out what they know about ceremonies.
3. Divide students into heterogeneous groups (encourage cooperative learning skills and division of labor).
4. Discuss with students the concept and history of ceremonies.
5. Review the definition of community and the various natural (flora, fauna, terrain, water, soil, weather, climate) and cultural assets (structures, architecture, transportation, neighborhoods, downtown business districts, government) that exist within a community.
6. Ask students to discuss with their groups and come to a consensus on what aspect of their community they feel deserves to be honored with a special ceremony.
7. Ask students to further research their choice using the reference materials provided (see Materials).
8. Ask students to design a ceremony that honors their choice and includes the basic elements of ceremonies such as the story behind what's being honored—food, music, and costumes.
9. Provide students with adequate time to create the elements of their ceremony and to practice its proceedings. (*Note:* Each cooperative group could create its own ceremony, or each could create one section of a whole-class ceremony.)
10. Special performance/celebration day. Don't forget to videotape the event. Provide audience with feedback forms to help assess students' work.
11. Engage students in a discussion on the activity's focusing questions.
12. Assess students' acquisition of knowledge and progress toward attaining the standards being addressed.
13. Celebrate the students' work with a special viewing of the video.

Task-Specific Assessment

(products, performances, tasks, tools [rubrics/checklists], anecdotal observations)

pre- and post-KWLs   ceremony products   ceremony performances   video
community feedback forms   anecdotal observations of teamwork and discussion times

Generalized-Standard Assessment

1.19 Research rubric
2.2 Problem-solving checklist
4.5 Continuity and Change checklist

STEP 2

Identifying a Community Coordinator

Perhaps the most crucial person for ensuring the success of a local history program is the community coordinator who acts as a liaison between the school and the surrounding town or neighborhood. Generally, this person is a parent or a volunteer from a local organization such as R.S.V.P. (Retired Seniors Volunteer Program).

Whoever is chosen, the person should be well acquainted with elders and community members and be aware of, or at least eager to find out, the skills and talents those elders have to offer. Additionally, the community coordinator should be informed about the workings of the school such as classroom schedules and subject areas that can dovetail with the skills and stories the elders have to offer.

Studying community transforms every community member into an expert. A parent shares traditional ranching skills at Chester Heritage Fair in Chester, Montana. Photo courtesy Montana Heritage Project.

Unfortunately, many elders have limited exposure to children nowadays, perhaps their only images being the unfavorable portrayals typically viewed on television. Consequently, elders sometimes need assurance that their visit will be safe and appreciated. In choosing an effective community coordinator, be sure that he or she has a warm and easygoing personality so that elders and others will feel safe coming into what is, for them, a foreign environment.

Most adults, particularly elders, rarely have an opportunity to participate in the life of their local school. Many feel that they are not needed or wanted as part of the curriculum being taught. We have learned through experience, however, that once elders are invited to share their stories and skills, they are delighted at the rare opportunity to be at the center of children's attention. A skillful community coordinator can help older people feel comfortable and at ease in the often frenetic environment of contemporary schools.

Following are a series of forms that will be helpful to the community coordinator in facilitating a local local history project. The "Community Resource Checklist" outlines the process of identifying community members to participate and matching their skills with the needs of the project as defined by the teachers. Use the "What's Your Story?" questionnaires to list the stories, skills, and interests that community volunteers, parents, and even other children can share in the school. Complete the "Local History Overview Form" to show at a glance the content of the project to interested community members.

Carriers of Cultural Traditions
Elders as Teachers

The identification of "Elders" as culture-bearers is not simply a matter of chronological age, but a function of the respect accorded to individuals in each community who exemplify the values and lifeways of the local culture and who possess the wisdom and willingness to pass their knowledge on to future generations. Respected Elders serve as the philosophers, professors, and visionaries of a cultural community. In addition, many aspects of cultural knowledge can be learned from other members of a community who have not been recognized as elders, but seek to practice and teach local lifeways in culturally appropriate ways.

—From *Guidelines for Documenting, Representing, and Utilizing Cultural Knowledge,* via Alaska Native Knowledge Network

Community/School Resource Directory Checklist

In many localities, the area Chamber of Commerce or Town Hall has a Who's Who Community Directory. If such a publication exists in your locality, this is a perfect starting point. If not, create one using this checklist.

1. Meet with teachers to find out the specific stories, talents, and skills their students have identified as important to learn and that can align with statewide learning standards. Activities might include bread making, crocheting, food growing and food preserving, birdhouse carpentry, local architecture—the list can extend as long as teachers' imaginations are deep.

2. Identify local resource people skilled in the areas that the teachers have specified. If a community resource directory does not already exist, this would be a perfect opportunity for students or community volunteers to create one. By their nature, these directories honor the skills and talent in any given locale.

3. Contact resource people in your area whose skills and experience align with student interests as described by participating teachers. If these community members are interested, and the match seems right, set up a time to conduct a personal interview to determine whether they would be suitable to work with a classroom of young students. A group of prospective community resource people could also be invited in for a luncheon to determine if there is a promising match.

   The coordinator should be aware that not everyone will be inclined or qualified—physically, socially, or emotionally—to handle the challenge of being with high-energy children. Because of the isolation of elders in modern society, many tend to feel uncomfortable, or are even averse, to the company of children.

   Use the "Community Resource Person Questionnaire" on page 52 to interview interested community volunteers. Be sure to give each interviewee a copy of the completed "Local History Project Overview Form" on page 58 to acquaint them with the project.

   Besides determining the story or skill a community member can share, the interview is also important for ascertaining whether someone is suited to participate in the often hectic pace of the average school. Through the interview, the community coordinator will be able to gain a much clearer sense of who will have the desire and patience to to be with eager students. Small groups of students led by adults may also do a home visitation to interview an elder.

4. Once this survey is done, compile the research into specific categories, such as by occupation (artists, farmers, homemakers, engineers, woodworkers/builders) or by skill (sewing and knitting, cooking and baking, arts and crafts, storytelling,). Now you have created your own community resource directory! Host a community/school celebration to honor the wealth of talent that exists in your community. Students can hand out free copies of the directory to all those who are listed.

5. Drawing from the directory, teachers can now choose the various resource people that they want to bring into their local history curriculum.

6. Meet with teachers to share the information gathered from the interviews. Decide together which community members would be most appropriate to invite, then set up a schedule of dates and times for them to participate.

What's Your Story?
Community Resource Person Questionnaire

Name ______________________________

Address ______________________________

Phone number ______________________________

Length of time in this area ______________________________

Profession, career skills ______________________________

Hobbies ______________________________

Interests ______________________________

Note: If no local community resource directory exists, you may want to bring along a camera to photograph the people being interviewed for inclusion in the directory.

1. Can you describe any unique stories, skills, and talents that you could share with children? Please explain.

2. Where was your place of birth? Please describe your family, childhood home, neighborhood, town, school, early years.

3. What were your major interests as a child (sports, hobbies, work)? Please describe some highlights from your childhood education.

4. In what ways has the world changed the most since you were a child? Describe how you feel about those changes.

5. What are your greatest hopes for bringing the school and community together to learn from one another in the future?

6. Do you have any other thoughts to share about making history come to life for children today?

7. What do you think children will gain from learning about the history of our community from elders and community members?

WHAT'S YOUR STORY?
Student Questionnaire

Name ______________________________

Address ______________________________

Phone number ______________________________

Length of time in this area ______________________________

Career choice ______________________________

Hobbies ______________________________

Interests ______________________________

1. Can you describe any unique stories, skills, and talents that you could share with other children? Please explain.

2. Where was your place of birth? Please describe your family, childhood home, neighborhood, town, school, life.

3. What are your major interests (sports, hobbies, work)?

4. In what ways has the world changed the most since you were born?

5. What are your greatest hopes and dreams for the future?

6. What would you most like to learn about your community (for example, nature studies, buildings, people, families, jobs)?

7. Do you have any other thoughts to share on learning about your community?

WHAT'S YOUR STORY?
Parent Questionnaire

Name ______________________________

Address ______________________________

Phone number ______________________________

Length of time in this area ______________________________

Profession, career skills ______________________________

Hobbies ______________________________

Interests ______________________________

1. Can you describe any unique stories, skills, and talents that you could share with children? Please explain.

2. Where was your place of birth? Please describe your family, childhood home, neighborhood, town, school, early years.

3. What were your major interests as a child (sports, hobbies, work)? Please describe some highlights from your childhood education.

4. In what ways has the world changed the most since you were a child? Describe how you feel about those changes.

5. What are your greatest hopes for bringing the school and community together to learn from one another in the future?

6. Do you have any other thoughts to share about making history come to life for children today?

7. What do you think your children will gain from learning about the history of the community from elders and community members?

Local History Program Overview Form

Title of Project

School Name

Purpose

Process

Volunteer Role

Culminating Event

Supporters

Contact

Local History Program Overview (*Sample*)

Title of Project

Getting to Know You: Connecting Students to the Wisdom of Elders

School Name

Peacham School

Purpose

To provide students opportunities to experience a genuine sense of place by connecting them to the real-life stories, skills, and knowledge of elders and other community members in the town of Peacham, Vermont.

Process

Local elders go into the classroom to share their stories and skills with the children. For those living in close proximity to the school, students can also visit elders at their homes, where appropriate.

Volunteer Role

We are asking each community participant to volunteer thirty minutes of their time to tell a story, share a skill, or engage students in some hands-on activity. Students will be prepared with questions specific to the skill or story that is shared.

Culminating Event

"Peacham Cultural Roots Celebration": Three months from now, parents, elders, and community members are invited to the school for student presentations, displays, and exhibits that demonstrate what they have learned from the project.

Supporters

Peacham Parents and Teachers Organization; school board; senior citizens' center; historical society

Contact

Thelma White, volunteer coordinator

SPIN THE LEADER
Role-playing the Community Coordinator

Standard(s) Being Addressed

2.2	Problem Solving	4.5	Continuity and Change
3.10	Teamwork	7.11	Systems: Analysis
4.1	Service		

Inquiry/Focusing Questions

If we were to create a ceremony that honored our community, what would that ceremony look like? What aspects of our community would it honor?

Who should be involved and how do we go about coordinating this ceremony?

How might we honor the ways our surrounding landscape impacts our community?

How might we honor the ways our community impacts our surrounding landscape?

Why is there such a strong connection between the natural heritage and cultural heritage of a community?

Topic

Preparing the community coordinators

Learning about cultural diversity, community resources, community service, and local political processes through role-playing activities

Materials

The Wizard's Staff video, created in the previous activity

community resource lists

citizen and business directories of the local community

blank procedure outlines

Procedure

1. Contact prospective community coordinators and schedule a time for them to meet with you.
2. Invite students to attend the community coordinator meeting as community coordinator apprentices.
3. Preassess students individually using a blank procedure outline ("Step 1, Step 2, Step 3") to determine what they know about how community traditions evolve.
4. Meet with community coordinators, view *The Wizard's Staff* video, and explain that the goal of this project is to institute the students' ceremonies as one of the larger community's traditions.
5. Divide community coordinators and students into groups and, using the video, resource lists, and directories, ask each group to devise two plans: (1) a plan for recruiting community members to participate with the students in their community ceremonies and (2) a plan for getting these ceremonies adopted as official community traditions. (*Note:* Each group could develop a comprehensive plan for both goals or each could devise a plan that targets specific elements of the two goals.)
6. Ask community coordinator teams to share and coordinate their plans.
7. Ask community coordinator teams to implement their plans.
8. Engage students in a discussion on the activity's focusing questions.
9. Assess students' acquisition of knowledge and progress toward attaining the standards being addressed.

Task-Specific Assessment

(products, performances, tasks, tools [rubrics/checklists], anecdotal observations)

pre- and postprocedure outlines, plans 1 and 2

anecdotal observations of teamwork and discussion times

Generalized-Standard Assessment

- 2.2 Problem-solving checklist
- 4.1 Service checklist
- 3.10 Teamwork rubrics

A TRIBUTE TO THELMA WHITE

Learning from Elders: The Missing Link

The catalyst for our first major local history project was Thelma White, a committed, lively, intensely curious octogenarian. Thelma grew up in a world that, she acknowledges, is rapidly disappearing today: extended families and cooperative living were the norm; people worked where they lived and grew most of the food they ate; and the generations closely intermingled—elders were revered for their time-tested wisdom and vivid stories, which offered deep and lasting lessons to young and old alike.

Compact with the Past

After she retired as principal of the Peacham School, in Vermont's Northeast Kingdom, Thelma made her own compact with the past: to bring to life the stories and traditions of her childhood by re-creating them with schoolchildren in her hometown of Peacham. This work of connecting the generations through school, Thelma realized, is as valuable for elders as it is for children.

The demands of modern life have separated young from old: as their worlds drift farther apart, they have become increasingly isolated from one another. Thelma's dream was to connect these worlds again, to bring back to life a time when people treasured the power of place, nurtured close personal relationships with their neighbors on whom they depended, and sustained themselves from the very land under their feet.

Every project needs a spark plug. Thelma has been the one who bridged the generational gap in Peacham to helped ignite a powerful local history program at the Peacham School, which has inspired the whole community.

"Bringing elders into the lives of children is the missing link in our modern education system," says Thelma. She believes that leaving elders out of the curriculum is the greatest oversight of schools and

represents a huge loss in our collective memory that we may never be able to recover.

Because so many elders still covet their essential connection to nature, as well as the vital importance of traditions like storytelling to pass on memories, they hold the key for ensuring that both rural and urban communities enter the technological communications age with their history and customs intact.

"It is very important to try somehow to bring these two, the older and the younger, together again because there is a need to know your background, to know what your roots are in order to be secure when you go out into the world."

Importantly, Thelma adds that providing this link is crucial to the health of both old and young. "And the first thing you know, you're in love with this child, if you're an older person," she says in *Getting to Know You*, "because they have brought you joy, they've brought you a reason for living."

Elders: Living Testaments

Having lived her whole life in Caledonia County, Thelma comes from a generation that valued science and technology but realized that the power of sustaining strong personal relationships, caring for the land and family, and learning the practical skills of the natural world were equally important. These elders are living testaments, the carriers of this way of being for the upcoming generations to learn from.

Because so many elders still covet their essential connection to nature, as well as the vital importance of traditions like storytelling to pass on memories, they hold the key for ensuring that both rural and urban communities enter the technological communications age with their history and customs intact. As a retired teacher and principal and current school board member, Thelma believes that the wisdom embodied in the lives of our elders may very well be the same stories and skills we will need the most as we move into the twenty-first century.

Because of this strong commitment, Thelma is widely sought for advice on how to do this—how to bring elders into schools and how to prepare teachers, students, and schools for the meeting of the generations.

To us at Food Works, Thelma has been an inspiration to learn our local histories and the stories that live in and sustain the roots of our communities. Just as she inspires us, she brings spirit into the lives of those she touches, from children to adults to the elders of her generation.

The Untapped Living Curriculum

While Thelma is one shining example, we have come to see that there are people in every community who have these qualities to connect the life of a school to community life. Our communities include countless Thelma Whites—engineers, artists, bakers, potters, farmers, house builders, musicians, homemakers—whose lives have been filled with science, math, technology, and history. They are the untapped living curriculum—the natural teachers from all walks of life who are living among us now, waiting to be asked to participate in the lives of children, to feel the joy of being with a curious youngster.

So we honor Thelma for all the gifts that she shares so freely with us. She has been a teacher, a friend, an aunty, a birder, a historian, and a horticulturalist. And above all, she has been a spiritual voice that fills our hearts with a deep love.

It is our hope that as people from other communities see this documentary and read these stories, they will also become inspired to share their wisdom and life experiences with younger children whose curiosity for learning and life is so strong.

STEP 3

Preparing Students

Interviewing community members, particularly elders, combined with activities such as mapmaking provide excellent opportunities for assessing students' current knowledge of the people and issues they will be learning more about throughout this unit of local study. Student performance in the initial assessment tasks, activities, and tools described in this chapter should be thoroughly documented in their student portfolios. This documentation serves as an ideal baseline from which to measure student learning at the end of the project. On completion of the unit, students should perform these same activities again to assess their growth in knowledge and skills.

Share Circles: A Suggested Preassessment Activity

The time-honored practice of a KWL—asking the class what they already *Know* about their community, what they *Want* to learn, and, at the completion of the unit, what they have *Learned*—allows students to express what they do and do not know at the outset of the learning process. It also provides an opportunity to discover misconceptions and biases they might have. KWLs can be conducted in a variety of ways. One effective way to conduct a KWL, while also introducing students to the art of interviewing, is to have students participate in share circles.

After completing a preassessment share circle, the teacher will have a much clearer sense of students' perceptions of people living in their community—their lives and the challenges that they face. This information will be invaluable in guiding teachers where to focus their unit of study in the community.

In the sample question-and-answer share circles on the following pages, note how clarifying questions are crucial to encourage students to think deeply about the study topic and specify what they would like to investigate.

Using a flip chart, students can write down, or the teacher can write for students not yet able to write, specific questions that they will ask in their interviews with an elder or community member. The answers that the children receive and record become learning evidence for their portfolios.

The Golden Rule of Share Circles

Since the earliest human settlements, people have gathered in circles to speak and listen to one another. The golden rule of this original, intimate form of grassroots democracy is to honor each person's compassion and innate wisdom about the ways of the world. Many teachers prefer to use talking sticks or some other symbolic object as a means for children to cooperatively share speaking time in a large group. With talking sticks, the group remains silent while the person who is speaking holds the stick and, when finished, passes the stick on to the next speaker.

Sample Share Circle Question 1

Teacher: If we invited elders and other community members into this classroom, what would you like to learn from them?

Possible Response: I want to know what life was like back when they were little.

Teacher (clarifying question): Tell me more—what would you like to know about their childhood?

Possible Response: I'd like to know what their home was like, what kinds of food they ate, if they watched television.

Sample Student Questions (Topic 1: Food)

1. What did you eat when you were a child?
2. Where did your food come from?
3. How did your family cook?
4. What kinds of diet did you have? (meals, recipes)

Sample Student Questions (Topic 2: Clothes)

1. What kinds of clothes did you wear?
2. Where did you get your clothes from?
3. How did you stay warm in winter?
4. What did you wear to school?

Sample Share Circle Question 2

Teacher: What stories would you like to hear from elders and others living here?

Possible Response: Stories about when they were children.

Teacher (clarifying question): What kinds of stories exactly? What things would you like to find out about when they were children?

Possible Response: I'd like to hear my neighbor, Mrs. Kitchel, tell me the same bedtime stories that her grandmother told her when she was my age.

Other story topics might include school stories of long ago, "a day in the life of . . . ," music and entertainment, great weather events of the past, popular books and literature, technology (radio, cars, the dawn of television, life before computers), outdoor life (on the farm, garden, sugaring, manual labor).

Sample Student Questions (Topic 3: School)

1. How big was your school?
2. What subjects did you study?
3. How far did you travel to school and how did you get there?
4. Who were your teachers?

Sample Student Questions (Topic 4: Work)

1. What kind of work did you or your father and mother do?
2. What was your pay?
3. What kinds of machines did they have at work?
4. Was the work harder then than it is now?

Sample Share Circle Question 3

Teacher: What do you suppose happens to people when they get older?

Possible Response: They get sick; they can't take care of themselves; they might be hungry and need food. [*Note:* These are actual responses from children in the *Getting to Know You* documentary video.]

Teacher (clarifying comment): OK, good. I wrote down on the flip chart what we think right now about what it's like to grow old. Let's invite some elders in and hear what they have to say and see what we can learn with this as our starting point.

Sample Share Circle Question 4

Teacher: In what ways can we be of help to others in our town?

Possible Response: We can do things for them; help them out on errands.

Teacher (clarifying question): Can you be more more specific? Give an example of how you can help an elder or relative you know.

Possible Response: I'd like to help my grandmother rake her leaves and plant her garden.

Role-playing: Preparing to Interview Elders

After the class has assembled their list of questions, students will need to practice interacting with and interviewing elders and other community members. Role-playing is one very effective way for students to learn listening and interviewing skills.

First, review the Listening Skills and Interviewing Skills Checklists in Appendix B so that students have a clear understanding of what makes a good listener and interviewer. Next, the teacher can model an interview with another adult to demonstrate both good and bad interviewing techniques. Ask the students to identify what worked and didn't work in the interview. Next, the students can interview each other and discuss and critique their own interviewing styles. This simple exercise works wonders in teaching children lifelong listening and interviewing skills.

Continuous Assessment

Throughout the course of the unit, there are multiple opportunities to do ongoing assessment to identify areas where students are making progress as well as those areas where they need additional coaching and support. Documenting these share circles at the outset of the unit, and then documenting students' responses to these same questions at the end of the project as a postassessment, will dramatically demonstrate the learning that has taken place throughout the course of study.

Videotaping is a particularly powerful means of assessing student learning because the video itself becomes part of the story of what has been learned. Other popular forms of documentation include photographs, student drawings, and journals. In most cases, participating community members are as impressed by what they gained from the experience as the students are about what they learned from their community.

Additional Preassessment Activity Ideas

Arts

Students draw a map of what they think their neighborhood, town, or village was like sixty to ninety years ago; include buildings, stores, roads, the natural landscape.

Students draw a picture of what they think a typical classroom was like sixty to ninety years years ago.

Language Arts

Depending on their age, students write about a day in the life of a child in the early part of the twentieth century.

Take-home Assignment

With their family, students facilitate a series of questions on their perceptions of what life was like sixty to ninety years ago in the community. What would each family member like to know from a local elder that the student could ask?

A Word About Developmentally Appropriate Local History Activities

It's no secret that our sense of history becomes deeper and more refined as we grow older. The stark contrast between different age groups' perceptions of and appreciation for history is clearly evident when we compare students in different grades.

In a typical schoolwide local history project, for example, it would not be unusual for eighth graders to want to interview historians and elders and construct a scale model of the streets, natural landmarks, or neighborhoods of their community in ages past. Fourth graders may have less patience to conduct interviews and construct an accurate historical model but may be more interested in reconstructing their favorite buildings in town as accurately as possible and investigating the history of the buildings that they have modeled.

Writing journal entries from the viewpoint of a child from a different historical era is one assessment activity that can measure a student's learning as the local history unit progresses.

At the kindergarten and first grade level, however, children rarely consider how historical events have shaped their community today and may find it difficult to systematically focus their questions on anything beyond the anecdotal concerning what may have happened before they were born. Therefore, a well-conceived local history unit for the early years will allow for a wide variety of questions and areas of interest to be explored with less emphasis on whether the topics fall strictly under the category of history.

Next Steps

With the class as a whole, brainstorm project ideas and activities that the students would like to pursue based on their responses to the questions during Share Circle. List these ideas on a flip chart, then refine them to create clear and focused lesson plans aligned to the standards using Form C on page 33.

EIGHTY YEARS YOUNG
Role-playing a Local Elder

Standard(s) Being Addressed

2.2	Problem Solving	4.1	Service
3.10	Teamwork	4.5	Continuity and Change

Inquiry/Focusing Questions

What does it mean to be an elder? At what point does one become an elder?

Who are our community elders? Which elder(s) has lived here the longest?

What stories do our elders have to tell about our community?

What ways have they seen our surrounding landscape impact our community?

What ways have they seen our community impact our surrounding landscape?

What are their thoughts about the connections between the natural heritage and cultural heritage of our community?

Topic

Preparing the community elders

Learning about cultural diversity, community resources, and community service through role-playing activities

Materials

tape recorders and blank cassettes

interview logs (composition booklets work well)

video recorder

blank Venn diagrams

Procedures

1. Ask your community coordinator(s) to contact community elder volunteers and schedule a time for them to meet with you and your students. Ask your community coordinator(s) to explain to the elders that the purpose of this initial meeting is for them to meet the teacher and students, share a little about their lives, and share with the students what they think are the most significant examples of local continuity and change they've seen during their lifetime. Ask your community coordinator(s) to also

explain to them that this initial meeting will be used by the students to help generate ideas for future interviewing and mentorship projects that the students and elders will ultimately work on together.

2. Preassess students individually using a blank Venn diagram to determine what they know about community elders by having them compare/contrast themselves with elders.
3. Discuss with the students that the purpose of their initial session with the local elders is to meet them and learn more about their community through the stories the elders will be sharing. Remind students that they will be using the information they hear to plan subsequent interviews and mentorship projects with these elders.
4. Meet with community elders, introduce elders and students to one another, and then divide community elders and students into groups.
5. Ask the elders to share with the students a little about their lives and stories they have that tell of the continuity and change they've witnessed within the community. Remind students to record, in words or pictures, the elders' stories in their interview logs (or tape-record) along with any interview/project ideas they generate while listening to the elders' stories. (*Note:* Each group could listen to all the elders' stories by having the elders rotate from group to group, or each group could record the story of its elder, and then work with the other groups to combine the different elders' stories.)
6. Provide elders with feedback forms for gathering information on how they felt about their initial session with the students, what they think did and didn't go well, and what they feel they need to prepare for the interviewing and mentorship projects they'll be working on with the students. Share the feedback forms with your community coordinator(s), and if necessary, ask him or her to schedule a follow-up meeting for you and the elders.
7. Engage students in a discussion on the activity's focusing questions.
8. Assess students' acquisition of knowledge and progress toward attaining the standards being addressed.

Task-Specific Assessment

(products, performances, tasks, tools [rubrics/checklists], anecdotal observations)

pre- and post-Venn diagrams   interview logs

anecdotal observations during story (group) time with elders

Generalized-Standard Assessment

3.10 Teamwork rubric

4.1 Service checklist

6.6 Being a Historian rubric/checklist

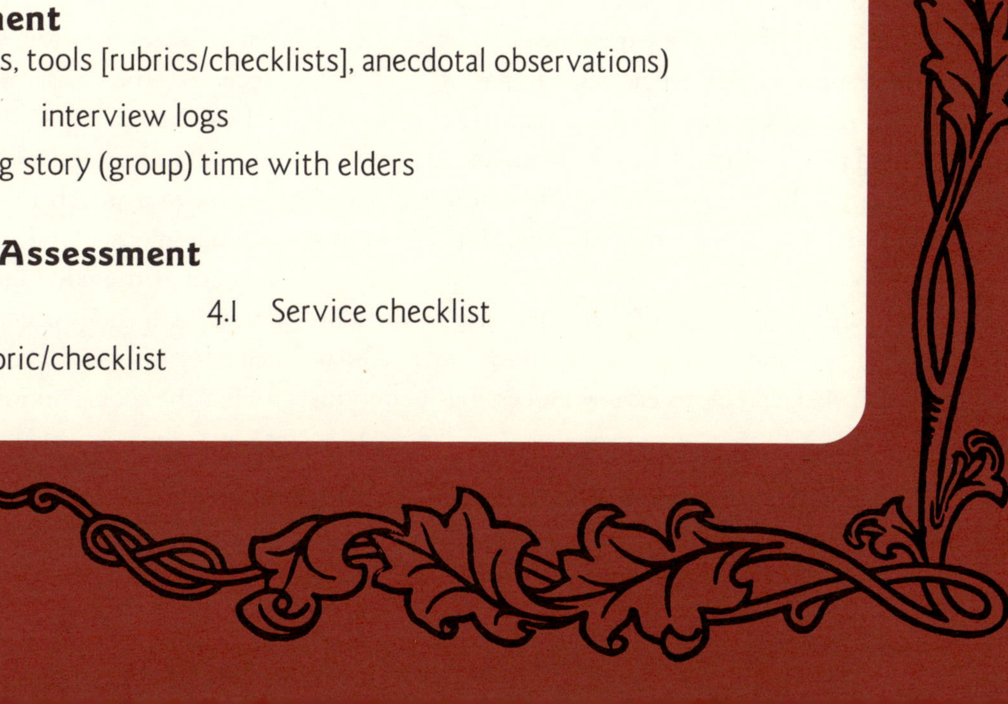

FROM ALASKA

From Passive Observer to Experiential Learner

Parents and Children Learning Traditional Knowledge and Skills Together

by Esther Ilutsik

Why is it that when we, the Native people, bring up the idea of teaching the local indigenous culture in the school, we still hear comments like, "They should just teach it at home if they think it is so important." Many of the things we want our children to learn we, as Native parents, haven't learned. So how can we teach the cultural knowledge that we feel is important to our children when we have not been taught these things ourselves?

Many educators or even community members do not realize that we have a generation of parents who have not had the opportunity to engage in activities that would make their culture more meaningful to them. They sense that it is important and know that it is something that will help their own children gain a better understanding of who they are. They see it and hear about it, but since they have not experienced and practiced it themselves, they are not able to pass it on.

Therefore we, as educators at the university and public school levels, have an added responsibility—the responsibility of educating those who missed out on these traditional learning opportunities.

Interviewing is the most popular way of collecting and documenting traditional Yup'ik knowledge. The interview process has many different variations. For example, public school teachers have students interview Elders on subject areas that they are interested in. This process is usually teacher-directed and, most often, the information gathered is limited due to barriers in communication. But even this process does not take into consideration the type of information that would be collected and documented if the participants were able to actually experience it.

For example, there is an art to gathering the edible roots from bush mice. You hear about how mouse food is gathered. You learn that it is gathered during a certain part of a season. You may even have the opportunity to see it, but you have not had the opportunity to engage in this activity to see how it is done. It is like looking into another world, because when questions are asked of the Elders, they share what they know, but in many cases they forget to share significant details because they assume everyone already knows those things.

On one such occasion, we interviewed and recorded as much information as we could about edible mouse food from our Elders: what the names of the edible roots were, what they might taste like, the process used in preparing them for meals, and even having the Elders attempt to draw what the roots and tubers looked like. It was then decided that we should go out and gather these edible roots.

During the field trip we, the students, observed the Elders in action. They knew exactly where to go and we followed. We observed as they looked for a certain area with the types of plants that they knew the mice would cache. Then they would look into the grass. When questioned, they said, "Oh, we're looking for telltale signs of mice. You see they have little roads in the grass." So we, the learners, looked and to our amazement saw all these little highways. Then they started taking little steps and moving up and down. When questioned, they said, "Oh, we are feeling for a spongy area. If it feels spongy it might be the mouse nest or it might be the food cache." Then, when a mouse cache was found, the tools were taken out: an uluaq, a bag and even some bits of dried fish and crackers. The nest had to be cut in a special way so that the Elders would be able to leave it as naturally as they had found it. After the edible roots were taken they were replaced with dried fish and cracker crumbs, and thanks was given.

When learning passively from our Elders, we are able only to bring limited information and insights back into the classroom; but through participation in the actual field of activity, the information takes on much greater validation and meaning.

In experiencing and practicing the gathering of edible mouse food, we were able to document a great deal more information than we would have if we had just relied on the interviews. We, as educators, had acquired information that was validated by our own experience and practice. When learning passively from our Elders, we able only to bring limited information and insights back into the classroom, but through participation in the actual field activity, the information takes on much greater validation and meaning.

As teachers and educators, we are responsible for sharing the information we gather with students who want to learn more about their culture, as well as other individuals who are within the present school system and community. What avenues are available to share such information so that others may also benefit from this knowledge?

There are many new materials being developed for integration into the school environment that address the approaches to the teaching described above. Specific ideas and suggestions are outlined in the Alaska Standards for Culturally Responsive Schools, available through the Alaska Native Knowledge Network/Alaska Rural Systemic Initiative (AKSRI). One of the initiatives of AKSRI involves implementing "Native Ways of Knowing" into school teaching practices, including documenting traditional cultural knowledge and incorporating it into curriculum using experiential methods. As a result of this initiative, many new materials are now being developed and integrated into the regular classroom. Schools are beginning the process of becoming grounded within the local culture.

We, as Elders, educators, and teachers, are very optimistic that the educational environment within the Western schools will change so that learning will fit the needs of the students; so that teachers coming into the area will have an understanding of and sensitivity to the local culture; and so that we will begin to see some positive changes for our people and communities.

It truly is an exciting time in education!

Excerpts reprinted from "Traditional Yup'ik Knowledge—Lessons for All of Us" in Sharing Our Pathways, *vol. 4, issue 4, a newsletter of the Alaska Rural Systemic Initiative.*

STEP 4

Preparing Elders and Community Participants

It is no secret that in today's world, opportunities for bringing the generations together are few. As a rule, people of different ages are isolated from one another during the course of a normal day: children are at school, parents are at work, elders stay at home or live separately at retirement centers. Only on the occasional holiday does a typical family find the time (or make the extra effort) to bring the old and young together.

In modern society, elders in particular feel isolated and alone. The places where children work and play during the day—schools—in general offer little opportunity for elders to come and spend time, even though their taxes are most likely helping to pay for those schools. Indeed, most taxpayers have little or no connection to, or knowledge of, the schools that their taxes support, nor are they likely to understand the way schools work or the outcomes of the schooling process.

At the same time, many elders are often reluctant to leave their homes and enter the world of today's modern school. For some, their limited exposure to children makes them anxious about being with all that exuberant energy. Others feel that they have nothing important to share.

And yet, once elders and community members have been invited into a school, shared a meal, and been honored for telling their life stories, they often feel a deep joy and appreciation at being with children again. Our experience has shown that after these seeds are planted, the desire for more contact grows, whether it be elders visiting children in school or children visiting elders in their homes.

Mindful of this alienation between young and old, and the great potential that lies in overcoming it by involving children and elders in a local history project, the community liaison plays a crucial role in making personal contact with community members and gradually bringing them into the school.

A Community Tea

A school-sponsored tea, breakfast, or modest lunch with the community has proven to be successful in launching a place-based learning project.

Food truly does work to bridge the gap between generations and ease the awkwardness that strangers often feel when they first meet. The project organizers can also use a community tea to find out about potential participants and decide who would be best suited to work with students in the school.

Following is a step-by-step outline of how the community coordinator and students can work together to organize this kick-off event.

1. Identify community members and elders to invite to the tea based on the theme of the local history unit, the topics to be addressed, and student interest areas.
2. Have students create personalized invitations and mail them to invitees.
3. Have students prepare a list of questions they would like to ask the guests, such as: What was school like when you were a child? What was your favorite subject in school? What do you like to do outdoors?
4. Have students prepare food and refreshments for the event.
5. As many elders may not be able to drive themselves to the school, arrange transportation beforehand, such as a school van or parent volunteers willing to provide transportation.
6. At the tea, breakfast, or lunch, assign one child or a group of children to each guest to make certain he or she is comfortable. It is essential that each visitor to the school feels safe and treated with respect.
7. Have students interview the guests, and the guests in turn should be encouraged to ask children questions, such as: Where do you live? Do you have any brothers or sisters? What do you like to study? What are some of your favorites things to do outside school? Do you have your own garden?
8. If possible, videotape the event or take photographs to include in the project portfolio.
9. Shortly after the tea or breakfast, have students write and send thank you cards to each participant, noting special conversations and other highlights of the day.
10. Have students transcribe interviews of elders and draw pictures, which can be compiled in a book and read to other children as a way of passing on these stories to all children.
11. Have teachers conduct a postassessment to find out what the students have learned and what they're curious to learn more about. For example, if a visitor talked about crochet work and making blankets, the class may want to invite her back to make a class blanket that could then be given to someone in the community as part of a service-learning project.
12. Once the community volunteers are chosen, give each the "Community Volunteer Story/Activity Outline" on page 78. This guide will prepare them to share their knowledge and experience with children.

Suggestions and Tips for Community Volunteers in Classrooms

Community members have so much to share with students, and their time is most valuable when they prepare short stories or presentations for a class. Because children, especially young children, tend to have short attention spans, the presentation need not be long. Successful presenters offer the highlights first, then ask for questions and let the questions set the direction. Visual aids are helpful: they jar the memory—and children love them!

- Keep it short.
- Have a visual aide (a photo, artifact, or piece of memorabilia—such as a dress or jewelry).
- Ask for questions.
- Ask the children questions: what they think life was like way back when, what they'd like to know.
- Share a simple story from the past: a school story, a family story.
- If possible, do something with the children: cooking, knitting, sewing, making jam or jelly—the lost arts of living in place.

Community Volunteer Story/Activity Outline

Title

Introduction

Main Points

Photos and Artifacts

Student Questions

Summary

Activity (where applicable)
Estimated length of activity:

Materials:

Procedure:

Community Volunteer Story/Activity Outline (*Sample*)

Title

Engineering a Birdhouse

Introduction

"My name is Fred Fortin. I haven't always been a bus driver. I'm actually a retired engineer. Do you know what an engineer does?"

Student response, discuss

Describe designing process, math, technology of building bridges

Main Points

"Today, we are going to engineer and build a birdhouse."

Students draw their own plans for building a birdhouse.

Show students my design of birdhouse.

Explain the process and materials needed for building a strong, efficient birdhouse.

Next class: We'll build our own birdhouse working in small groups.

Photos and Artifacts

Photos of bridges and other structures I've designed

Student Questions

Summary

Emphasize importance of using these skills together—measurement, design, planning, execution—to solve problems in the real world.

Next visit: solve the problem of designing houses for birds in the winter

Activity (where applicable)

Estimated length of activity:
45 minutes

Materials:
Precut ½-inch pine boards, finishing nails, hammers, wood glue, sandpaper, pliers

Procedure:
Refer to blueprint design.

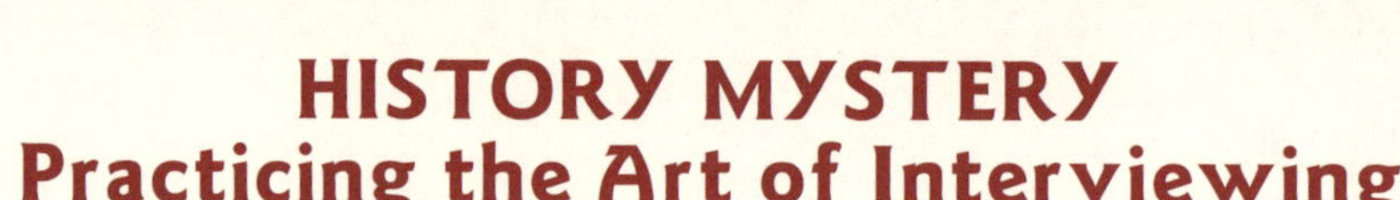

HISTORY MYSTERY
Practicing the Art of Interviewing

Standard(s) Being Addressed

1.18	Information Technology	4.1	Service
1.19	Research	4.5	Continuity and Change
3.10	Teamwork	6.6	Being a Historian

Inquiry/Focusing Questions

What was our community like a century ago?

What was it like being a child in our community a century ago?

What stories might our community elders want to share about our community?

What changes in our community and surrounding landscape have our elders witnessed?

How do our elders feel about the relationship our community has with its surrounding landscape today compared to a century ago?

Topic

Preparing the students

Learning the art of interviewing, the skill of being a historian, and the value and wisdom of our elders

Materials

interview logs (composition books work well)

video recorder

Procedures

1. Preassess students individually through role-playing to determine preexisting interviewing skills. (*Note:* You might want to videotape these preassessment role-plays as a way to document student performance and provide concrete feedback to the students.)
2. Divide students into heterogeneous groups (encourage cooperative learning skills and division of labor). (*Note:* You might choose to have the students remain in the

groups they were in during the "Eighty *Years Young*" activity to maintain consistency.)

3. Review with students the definition of community and the various natural (flora, fauna, terrain, water, soil, weather, climate) and cultural assets (trades, architecture, transportation, neighborhoods, agriculture, industry, technology) that exist within a community.
4. Ask students to review with the class the information they gathered in their interview logs during the initial meeting they had with community elders.
5. Ask students to consider the information reviewed in Steps 3 and 4 and then develop a set of interview questions that they would like to follow up on with the elders.
6. Review with students the general patterns that emerged from your preassessment role-plays regarding general interviewing skills (e.g., clarity of questions, active listening skills). Prompt the students on skills to focus on during the role-playing they are about to engage in.
7. Ask each group to practice their interviews by having each group member take a turn being the interviewer, the elder, and the "critical friend" doing the observing and critiquing.
8. Ask students to share their thoughts on what it was like playing the various roles.
9. Assess students' acquisition of knowledge and skills and progress toward attaining the standards being addressed.
10. Schedule a time for the students to conduct follow-up interviews with the community elders.

Task-Specific Assessment

(products, performances, tasks, tools [rubrics/checklists], anecdotal observations)

pre- and post-role-plays   interview logs   video recording

anecdotal observations of teamwork and discussion times

Generalized-Standard Assessment

3.10 Teamwork rubrics

6.6 Being a Historian rubric/checklist

4.5 Continuity and Change checklist

FROM MONTANA

History, Done Locally

Montana Heritage Project Brings Towns' Pasts Alive—with the Help of Children

by John Stromnes

Michael Umphrey, ambulance driver, poet, educational theorist, and dreamer of dreams, still needs his day job.

Since its inception in 1994, he's been director of the Montana Heritage Project, a nonprofit, privately funded endeavor to put students to work in their own communities discovering stories of their past. Umphrey works out of an old Flathead Agency building transplanted to St. Ignatius, his hometown, where he also taught and worked as a school administrator for years. He has a master of fine arts degree in creative writing from the University of Montana and is forty-eight years old.

Equipped with tape recorders, notebooks, video cameras, healthy curiosity, and good will, Montana Heritage Project students in small towns all across Montana are documenting the true riches of the Treasure State—its cultural past, Umphrey said.

"The idea behind the project is deceptively simple. We encourage classes to take their own community as the subject of serious academic study," he said.

"As schools become more community centered, communities start to become more education centered. The young and the old work together to understand their history. Kids are motivated. Teachers are invigorated. Schools are revitalized," Umphrey said.

He reflected a moment.

"This project has a delightfully subversive edge because it changes the relationships between teachers and their communities," he mused.

What has developed into the Montana Heritage Project had its start in conversations between philanthropist Art Ortenberg of Condon (the husband and business partner of clothes designer Liz Claiborne) and James Billington, librarian of the Library of Congress in Washington, D.C.

Ortenberg told Billington there was much to value in Montana. But he was concerned that Montana was losing its sense of self. Rural ways of life were dying; familiar, trusting relationships were disappearing; communities were losing their identity in the face of sweeping economic and social change.

They convened a statewide conference of stakeholders in Montana's culture and history and invited Alan Jabbour, director of the American Folklife Center for the Library of Congress, to suggest a framework that would involve students, teachers, and others in small communities in a collaboration to preserve Montana's heritage while there was still time. Funding was $200,000 a year and Ortenberg promised a long-term commitment.

At a meeting in Helena, Jabbour proposed engaging students in the living history of their own communities by convincing residents to tell their stories to students, who would document and preserve these stories in forms of their own choosing, guided by their teachers.

The idea behind the project is deceptively simple. We encourage classes to take their own community as the subject of serious academic study.

—Michael Umphrey, Director of the Montana Heritage Project

Umphrey was casting about for a new career after quitting his job as a school administrator at St. Ignatius. The fractious fights of small-town school politics had become exceedingly trying, and he wanted a new career. His background in education, his literary skills, and his abiding interest in Montana's heritage helped him get the job.

The Heritage Project has grown slowly but steadily under his leadership, gradually involving teachers, students, and elders from across the state. Heritage projects have been completed in Bigfork, Broadus, Chester, Columbus, Corvallis, Fort Benton, Libby, Pryor, Red Lodge, Roundup, St. Ignatius, Simms, and Townsend.

Sometimes the heritage of a small town is not all sweetness and light, as student researchers in Roundup discovered when they learned about the influence of the Ku Klux Klan in their community not so many years ago.

Of course, not all research projects are so disquieting. In Corvallis, students spent Saturdays in the Ravalli County Museum and started a "photo bazaar" (a collection of several hundred historical photos) to recruit community elders to share their stories.

In Libby, students documented logging practices of the past—and of the present, by visiting ongoing logging operations.

In Bigfork, 104 students in a freshman English class read *A River Runs Through It,* by Norman MacLean, and then organized an "expedition" to explore places where MacLean had lived, worked, and fished along the Blackfoot River. They even had a fly-fishing seminar.

Later, a core group of students did intensive interviews of Bigfork residents who were teenagers in the 1920s. Bigfork student Fabienne Fellows told a radio interviewer: "This has become more than a project. It has become a relationship."

Meanwhile, Umphrey and the Heritage Foundation have received national attention. Umphrey has been asked to speak to groups in Alberta, Kentucky, Oregon, and Tennessee, and educators from eighteen states have subscribed to the project newsletter.

Former U.S. Secretary of Education Richard W. Riley has addressed their annual teacher institute in Great Falls, where he congratulated teachers for their efforts to explore new efforts for American educators. The annual institute is open to educators from throughout Montana who want to learn more about community-centered teaching. Participating students have also been acknowledged for making original contributions to Montana's cultural heritage. They have donated their research to the state of Montana for permanent preservation in the Montana Historical Society archives.

"This project is like what used to happen with barn-raising efforts," Montana Governor Marc Racicot told teachers at their annual winter summit conference in Helena. "People contributed to an effort, and out of it came a melding of ideas and souls that could not be produced in any other way and was probably the most enduring aspect of the joint effort."

Umphrey said much the same thing in a different voice. "We're celebrating Montana's small, rural communities."

Adapted with permission from a feature article from The Missoulian.

STEP 5

Community Members Teach, Share, and Learn with Students

This step of the local history learning process involves community-based learning projects that students are involved in both inside and outside the classroom. Engaging students with community members is the essence of the program. Once the community resource people and the children become familiar with one another, their anticipation and excitement for learning grows in leaps and bounds.

As this intergenerational learning unfolds, new information will naturally be uncovered, relationships will be formed, and gifts will be shared.

Sample Local History Projects

The sample local history projects described here, all developed in schools around Vermont in coordination with Food Works staff, are grouped under the three local history areas we have identified in the *Getting to Know You* documentary.

Stories and Local History

Food and Gardening

The Environment and Crafts

These three categories are one possible way to organize community resources. It is by no means a comprehensive list. Additional themes could include clothing, schooling, entertainment and recreation, religion, transportation, industry, and the performing and fine arts.

On the following pages are descriptions of several local history projects as examples of the wide range of learning opportunities available for exploring the history of the surrounding community.

Stories and Local History

The local history thematic units being explored in the classroom provide a ready-made focus for community members to share their stories. Community resource people can bring in specific photos, artifacts, and stories for a presentation according to the themes identified by the teacher.

A Weekly Classroom Event: Community Heritage Day

Ideally, once storytelling is introduced into the curriculum, it will not be a once-a-year enrichment for students but will become a permanent part of the classroom experience. Many classrooms boast their own "Elders' Corner," which is set aside especially for seniors to come in each week to share stories on specific topics the class has determined beforehand.

An effective means for establishing storytelling as a permanent feature of students' learning experience is the KWL approach: find out what students already *Know* about a given topic; list everything that they *Want* to know; and at the end of each unit, determine what they have *Learned*.

One key goal of studying local history is for students to collect and preserve the stories and traditional knowledge that is being transmitted to them on an ongoing basis. To ensure continuity of the community stories within the curriculum, there must be a set of developmentally appropriate methods for students to document what they experience from the stories that they hear. The youngest students can sketch or paint, for example. Older students can write and illustrate their stories. And still older students can photograph and videotape interviews and create local documentaries. All these methods lend themselves to strengthening the cultural lifeline passed down through the generations.

It takes time for any new project to become established as a tradition that students can look forward to. When these documentation methods are intentionally conducted from year to year as part of a continuum of the schoolwide curriculum, they will become a permanent element of the community's living history. To formally incorporate this into the structure of the academic calendar, a regular time slot will need to be set up dedicated exclusively to documenting community stories. With a planned time for community resource people to visit every week, for example, students will come to expect and look forward to their weekly in-class "field trips" reexperiencing the history of their community through the voices of their elders.

Once this schedule has been set up, then a consistent framework of student expectations can be built using checklists or rubrics as assessment tools. Examples of rubrics and checklists can be found in Appendix B. These assessment tools can be used consistently so students understand exactly what to concentrate on during their sessions with community guests.

As an additional part of the assessment process, students should be encouraged to keep a community history portfolio, documenting guests and their stories through art and drawings and explaining the morals that these stories offer.

Together, the class can follow their curiosity by pursuing these stories even further. Through community outings, students can see for themselves the buildings, foundations, cemeteries, and artifacts of earlier settlements they learned about in the elders' stories.

These activities in turn stimulate other questions. Answers to good questions inevitably deepen any inquiry into understanding local history and a sense of place. Through the ongoing work of collecting community stories, children's curiosity is kindled and a respect and appreciation for the hidden stories in the lives of elders is nurtured. After learning directly from community seniors, children will now pause and ask themselves, whenever seeing an elder, "Hmm, I wonder: What's your story?"

Ten Benefits of Storytelling

1. Stories sustain an oral tradition that used the spoken word to instruct and stimulate the imagination.
2. Stories often have a message—a moral or lesson. In this way they transmit held values in an easy-to-understand way.
3. Stories preserve the culture for future generations. They pass on information about events and traditions that would otherwise be forgotten.
4. Stories reconnect us to indigenous ways where children learned directly from elders who taught—and even disciplined—through stories. They return elders to their rightful place: passing on their knowledge to children and reconnecting the lifeline between generations. Stories encourage a deep appreciation of the lives and experiences of elders and other community members; they foster honor and respect for those members.
5. Stories demonstrate a holistic way of living and learning through cross-curriculum connections (language arts, history, communication skills, problem solving, science, appropriate technology) and provide specific local meaning to broad, generalized learning standards.
6. Stories inspire young children to read and learn about their local heritage.
7. Stories promote ideography: Children can make pictures of stories and use those pictures to retell the stories.
8. Stories enable children to appreciate antique photos, tools, bicycles, and cars, which gives them a context for understanding how technology has evolved.
9. Stories provide a benchmark for how different modern life is from the past, allowing listeners to reflect on continuity and change and discuss the many issues that come with progress.
10. Stories offer a context for community building and celebration and provide a sense of belonging; through their own storytelling, students can share what they have learned about their cultural roots with elders and other community members.

ONCE UPON A TIME
Making a Classroom Big Book of an Elder's Story

Standard(s) Being Addressed

1.18	Information Technology	4.1	Service
1.19	Research	4.5	Continuity and Change
3.10	Teamwork	6.6	Being a Historian

Inquiry/Focusing Questions

What memories do our elders have of growing up and living in our community?

What are our elders' favorite childhood stories they like to tell?

What stories do you think you will want to tell the children of your community when you are an elder?

What story might our elders tell of the changes they've seen in our community and surrounding landscape?

What lesson might our elders feel they want to pass on regarding our community's relationship with the land?

Topic

Learning the art and value of storytelling, the skill of being a historian, and the value and wisdom of our elders

Materials

tape recorder

camera

video recorder

variety of art supplies (crayons, markers, Cray-Pas, colored pencils, paint, paint brushes, tissue paper, construction paper, scissors, glue, yarn)

large, big book paper

blank affective surveys

Procedure

1. Preassess students individually using an affective survey to determine how students feel about telling and listening to stories.
2. Divide students into heterogeneous groups (encourage cooperative learning skills and division of labor).
3. Explain to students that community elders will be visiting to tell a story of their community's past and that their task will be to help each other remember the stories and then re-create the stories in the form of a big book(s).
4. Arrange to have someone present on the day of the event to videotape and take photographs of the storytelling and book writing, from beginning to end. (*Note:* The teacher might want to tape record the stories for later dictation and retelling.)
5. Invite community elders to spend time sharing their stories with the students. Inform them ahead of time of the general patterns that emerged from the affective preassessments to help them prepare for their day with the students.
6. Ask students to work together on re-creating the elders' stories in the form of a big book(s). (*Note*: Each group could create its own big book, or each could work on one part of a whole-class big book.)
7. Ask students to share their books with their classmates and the elders.
8. Arrange to have the students' big book(s) and a photo essay of the event prominently displayed somewhere in the community.
9. Engage students in a discussion on the activity's focusing questions.
10. Assess students' affect, acquisition of knowledge and skills, and progress toward attaining the standards being addressed.

Task-Specific Assessment

(products, performances, tasks, tools [rubrics/checklists], anecdotal observations)

pre- and postaffective surveys   video recording   photo essay   tape recordings
big books   anecdotal observations of teamwork and storytelling time

Generalized-Standard Assessment

3.10 Teamwork rubrics

4.5 Continuity and Change checklist

6.6 Being a Historian rubric/checklist

Food and Gardening

With the advance of industrial and now information technology, we have become increasingly separated from our instinctual connection to the land. Much of the ancient knowledge of what the land can produce—such as wild foods and herbal medicines—is being forgotten. As we awaken to the need to reclaim this disappearing heritage, we can still turn to the keepers of this knowledge—our elders—for guidance, instruction, and leadership on how to return to these sustainable ways. Intergenerational gardening is a way to both honor the wisdom of elders and give them a sense that their knowledge and experience is valued by the community.

Food is an ideal vehicle for crossing generations and opening a dialogue between elders and children. Because food production has played a role in sustaining the heritage of communities, it is imperative to involve elders—those in their seventies, eighties, and nineties—many of whom still remember the traditional skills of food growing, preservation, and seed saving as if they practiced them yesterday.

Gardening Over Time

Although almost every element of our day-to-day lives has changed dramatically over the past few hundred years, the practice of home and community gardening has withstood the winds of change. The practical skills and knowledge involved in this high art and applied science—feeding the soil, planting passed-down crop varieties, putting food up, and so on—have endured generation after generation, connecting us to the source of life itself.

Because of the ready availability of food today, however, we are no longer dependent on our daily labors to grow and prepare our own food. Eating is perhaps one of the most taken-for-granted activities in our modern world. But in listening to elders tell their stories, we can gain a new appreciation for how people were once intimate with every step of the food cycle, from seed to table. In many cases, it is the elders who know from their own experience the details of local food production. With little prompting, they can describe and demonstrate the best times to plant, how to fertilize, the basics of plant care, how to put food up, storage tips, cooking ideas, and more.

Many older Americans take for granted these agricultural experiences that they had as children and still carry with them today. Growing their own food is such an intimate part of their personal story that they barely recognize its value in a world that treasures speed and efficiency over the wisdom of the earth it-

Top Ten Reasons to Garden Across the Generations

1. Passes down real-life skills and traditional earth knowledge.
2. Creates a foundation for lasting friendships.
3. Reconnects to the traditional role of elders teaching children.
4. Demonstrates the interdisciplinary nature of food and its applicability for teaching across the curriculum and addressing academic standards.
5. Utilizes garden tools and techniques that older Americans have used in earlier decades.
6. Encourages research into seed preservation techniques of heirloom varieties.
7. Reconnects the generations to the land itself and the mysteries of nature.
8. Revitalizes the historic spirit of a community working together.
9. Provides opportunities for recounting stories of local horticultural history.
10. Revives the old practice of subsistence agriculture through cooperative work experiences.

self. As the modern world neglects those elders who hold that sacred knowledge, the elders themselves are forgetting the lessons and stories of the land that have shaped their lives.

There is so much wisdom and heart in the ancient teachings of the plants. It is rare to find a teacher these days that knows the old ways, who can touch into the genetic memory encoded in the plants and is enseeded in each of us as part of our memory banks.

—Rosemary Gladstar, *The Science and Art of Herbology*

Waiting in the wings of every community—in senior centers, retirement communities, or at home alone—are Americans with practical gardening experience who are able to share these stories and skills with young children. What better way for a child to learn how to nourish a plant than hand in hand with an elder?

Where to Begin

For teachers who would like to grow plants with students but lack confidence in gardening, an ideal starting point is building an intergenerational gardening team of elders, parents, and children.

As educators search for ways to inspire students, many find school gardening a perfect vehicle to teach traditionally separate subject areas. Gardening is a simple way to practice local history. Seasonal tasks like harvesting, food preservation, and cover cropping are ways to recover any community's living history. (For a complete guide on integrating youth gardens into school curriculum, see *Digging Deeper: Integrating Youth Gardens into Schools and Communities*, by Joseph Kiefer and Martin Kemple.)

A community heritage garden is a good starter garden because it draws on the unique history of a community, ideally using the authentic tools, techniques, and heirloom varieties of seeds from a particular time. The whole food cycle can be taught with elders drawing from their own experience, thus creating a rich curriculum that children will remember their whole lives.

BAKING WITH ELDERS
Turning Old Recipes into Fresh Bread

Standard(s) Being Addressed

3.10	Teamwork	6.6	Being a Historian
4.1	Service	7.1	Scientific Method
4.5	Continuity and Change	7.7	Measurement

Inquiry/Focusing Questions

Did the children living in our community a century ago say they disliked the same foods that children, today, say they dislike?

What foods were commonly eaten by people living in our community a century ago, and why?

Which foods did our community ancestors have to grow and make and which were they able to buy at a store?

What foods commonly eaten today might not be part of our community's diet a century from now, and why?

How does our understanding of where food comes from compare to our ancestors' understanding of where food came from?

Topic

Learning the traditional knowledge and skills of kitchen gardening, the skill of being a historian, and the value and wisdom of our elders

Materials

tape recorder
video recorder
required ingredients and kitchen utensils
interview log books (composition booklets work well)
blank concept webs

Procedures

1. Preassess students individually using a concept web to determine what students know about where food comes from.

2. Divide students into heterogeneous groups (encourage cooperative learning skills and division of labor). (*Note:* Each group could create their own food or meal, or each could work on one part of a whole-class dish.)
3. Ask students to brainstorm a list of general or specific types of foods they believe are traditional and that they would like to learn to make.
4. Provide elders with the list and ask them to select a food (traditional version) from the list that they would like to teach the students how to make.
5. Explain to students that community elders will be visiting to work with them on how to make one of the traditional foods or meals they listed and that their task will be to listen, observe, and help each other learn the process for when they make these same foods or meals for upcoming community dinners and local food shelf projects.
6. Arrange to have someone present on the day of the event to videotape and take photographs of the students and elders working together. (*Note:* The teacher might want to videotape or tape-record the elders' lessons to replay for the students later. Older students can be asked to record observations in their interview logs while working with the elders.)
7. Invite community elders to spend time preparing traditional foods with the students.
8. Set aside time for students and elders to share their dishes with one another.
9. Arrange to have a photo essay of the event prominently displayed somewhere in the community.
10. Engage students in a discussion on the activity's focusing questions.
11. Assess students' acquisition of knowledge and skills and progress toward attaining the standards being addressed.
12. Schedule follow up community dinners and local food shelf projects for the students to demonstrate their knowledge and apply their skills toward community service.

Task-Specific Assessment

(products, performances, tasks, tools [rubrics/checklists], anecdotal observations)

pre- and postconcept webs   interview logs

video recording (performance)   foods/meals (products)   photo essay

anecdotal observations of teamwork and time spent working with elders

Generalized-Standard Assessment

3.10 Teamwork rubrics   7.1 Scientific Method (observations)

The Environment and Crafts

Older people in our society grew up in a much slower paced world in which people tended to be more connected to the everyday cycles and rhythms of nature. In rural communities especially, this intimate relationship with nature was an essential means of survival: how to grow food, how to build and heat a house, how to make remedies for treating illnesses. In generations past, this ecology of living was the natural foundation that shaped people's physical, emotional, cultural, and spiritual lives.

As recently as one hundred years ago and still today in many places, tools—such as the hand water pump, the ice box, and the splitting mall—were basic and manageable. They directly connected people to the natural world rather than buffering them from it, as so many of our modern machines tend to do (computers and television, to name two). The rupture from the old ways of living with nature makes the passing down of these skills and traditions so imperative for our modern world.

Elders have a lifetime of experience of living in one place that can be readily passed on to children. Many elders are deeply attached to the land. Having grown up before the automobile, they walked and hiked their region as a matter of course.

Because of their wealth of experience, it is crucial that elders have ample opportunity to share their stories and walk in nature with children so that young people can also cultivate a love for and understanding of the land. When we walk with those with more outdoor experience than we have, we learn that this is not just an ordinary walk in the woods, but a walk with many beings. Elders can retrain our eyes to see and our ears to hear. This means, on one level, seeing the interdependence of all beings in our natural environment: that the plant, the insect, and the bird all have a purpose, a niche. What follows are sample projects for investigating the local natural heritage:

Mapmaking over Time

Modeling the Local Watershed: Indoor River: Building an Indoor River in the Classroom

Local Historic Interpretive Walking, Biking, and Driving Tours

Local Natural History Explorations

Traditional Crafts: Making Local History

Mapmaking over Time

Children love maps. In making their own local maps, students learn the cardinal directions (north, south, east, and west) and the location of natural landmarks and roads, plus the relative locations of houses, neighborhoods, and downtowns.

Making historical maps with students is an engaging and interesting way to learn about local history and involve area seniors and community members at the same time. The best book we know on the subject is David Sobel's *Mapmaking with Children*.

Making maps is an especially adaptable learning project because it can be a one-day activity, or it can span the entire school year. One easy mapmaking starter activity is for students to simply map out their place in the classroom. Next, they could draw a map of the route from school to their home, detailing the roads and paths they use to get to school and back every day. Another map could include directions to a secret hiding place, such as a fort.

Mapmaking is a wonderful way to involve elders in the school. Seniors can be asked to help children draw maps of the community from long ago, including old roads, foot trails, and buildings that have been torn down. To enlist more community involvement, there are many local people whose life work revolves around maps: planners, architects, designers, road builders. Some interpret and read maps, while others are involved in making and designing new and more accurate maps.

Each town clerk keeps maps of all taxpayers based on their lot sizes. Most people have maps of the lot that their house sits on. By contacting your city hall, you can acquire maps of your town from 50, 100, even 200 years ago that depict old roads and even the old names of houses and natural landmarks.

Students can compare and contrast changes in the community through historical mapmaking activities: How has the land changed? How has the natural heritage shaped the cultural heritage? How has the cultural footprint impacted the natural landscape?

Here are other suggested local maps that can be created with students:

- Schoolyard habitat map
- School map
- Town and state maps
- Walking maps for historic local tours
- Walking maps for nature tours
- Architecture map
- Wetlands map
- Herb map
- Ecological resource map: agricultural land
- Animal's-eye-view maps: deer's-eye-view map, squirrel's-eye-view map, and bird's-eye-view maps. For example, a map of how a bird views the land searching for its perfect habitat: shelter, food, a place to raise young. Imagine the bird heading south.
- Waterway map: stream, brook, river, pond
- Relief map: Purchase a topographical map detailing local elevations and make a three-dimensional relief map or a diorama made of cardboard.
- Historical maps: the area surrounding the school long ago
- Sector maps: Through interviews of elders, create 50-year-old and 150-year-old maps. How far back can you go? To indigenous movement through the area?
- Culminating map: multilayered map using mylars in a series of overlays
- Future map: What do we want our town to look like in 50 years? How do we get involved in planning, design, and development so that we all have a place on our local map?

Modeling the Local Watershed: Building an Indoor River in the Classroom

Modeling the local watershed in the classroom is an excellent hands-on way for students to learn about the ecology, geography, and social and natural history of where they live. In conducting local river-building projects with schools over the years, our staff has seen how students gain a sense of ownership of and belonging to their locale through researching and reconstructing their area's watershed.

More specifically, students learn the topography of their region, the source and mouth of major rivers and streams in the local drainage basin, and the potential point and nonpoint source pollution along the way.

Experiments in biology and chemistry conducted on the indoor river model are reformulated to be conducted in the outdoor rivers to compare data and develop hypothetical models for understanding the natural and human influences on the development and makeup of the area's rivers.

Equally important, the design and construction process offers opportunities for involvement of parents and community members in the life of the school while at the same time engaging students in research and documentation of their watershed to present to the community-at-large. By displaying a model of the drainage basin for the general public, students educate local residents about the major features of the watershed—past, present, and future. This allows the community to look at the big picture of their watershed—spatially and historically—in developing a regionwide vision for the rivers' long-term health.

Assembling an Indoor River

The Indoor River Book, a Food Works publication, presents a clear step-by-step guide for building an indoor aquatic habitat.

The following is a brief summary of the process, which generally takes one to two weeks to complete.

1. **Involving the Community.** After obtaining permission from the principal—and custodial staff—

solicit support and advice from other teachers, parents, friends, local colleges and universities, and environmental organizations. The collective knowledge of the surrounding community is an invaluable resource for everything from the local ecology and aquatic habitats to the fine points of design and construction.

2. **Involving Students.** Ask students to create rough maps of the area (drawing the major natural and human landmarks) and to list their top five questions about the local waterways, such as: What is the source of the river? What is its water quality? How has the river been used historically? What communities once lived along the river? These questions, grouped and prioritized, then become the driving force behind subsequent project activities. Take a field trip to the river you are planning to model in class.
3. **River Design.** Choose one section of the river to model. Draw the river to scale using graph paper (or an overhead projector), then trace the outline of the river on long butcher paper.
4. **River Assembly.** You will need the following materials to construct a model of the river: rubber pond liner, 3/4-inch plywood, and 1-by-4-inch pine boards. Trace the outline of the river from the butcher paper on the plywood. Using a jigsaw, cut the plywood along the traced line. Lay the rubber pond liner on top of the plywood and cut it to fit the plywood. Using a staplegun, staple the liner onto the plywood; this forms the river bed. Construct a frame out of the pine boards and screw the plywood onto this frame.
5. **River Source and Mouth.** The source of the river can be a 16-by-22-by-6-inch polyvinyl container with a hole on the side and a short tube attached to direct water into the rubber channel. The mouth of the river is generally a standard aquarium. Use a submersible pump in the aquarium to pump the water back to the source through a long flexible tube.
6. **Stocking the River.** Obtain water from a nearby river or stream to pour into the model. Stock the indoor river with local aquatic plants to keep the water clean, then gradually add local aquatic insects.

Historic Interpretive Walking, Biking, and Driving Tours

These tours highlight the natural and social history of the surrounding area. By working with local historians or the historical society plus area elders, small groups of students can research the social history of specific houses and neighborhoods in their area. What story does a house have to tell? We pass by houses every day, but little do we wonder what stories they have to tell.

House

- Who built it?
- In what year?
- How much did it cost?
- Where did the building materials come from?
- Where is the original title?
- Who has lived there? What was their role in the community? What did they do for work? Did they have any children?

Neighborhood

- What was community life like when the houses in this neighborhood were built?
- How did this neighborhood develop?
- What were the relationships of the people who lived here? Create a community web of histories of people who have lived in the neighborhood.

Community

- What historic events have happened here?
- When and where was the town charter signed? By whom?
- How did the town get its name?

Local History Research Project

Exploring Area Cemeteries

Here are sample questions that students can use to research in a local cemetery:

- Which cemetery has the oldest tombstone? What is the date? name?
- What do the names reveal about the origins of these settlers?
- Locate the tombstones of the key families who first settled here.
- What evidence is there of local families intermarrying?
- Graph the average age of people who were buried in the cemetery. Has life expectancy increased or decreased over time. Why or why not? Did men live longer or shorter than women?
- Did more children die premature deaths then than now? How many infants died compared to those who died over age one or two? What were the causes of death?

Local Natural History Explorations

Teaching natural history forms the foundation for a lifetime of understanding and appreciation of place-based education. Every community is filled with people who have a wealth of knowledge about the natural world—from birders to botanists to farmers to foresters to game wardens to hunters. Who can be called on to interpret the biodiversity of the natural landscape? By building on the natural curiosity of children, we can encourage them to choose careers that help to restore and protect our precious natural heritage.

Birding

A lifelong passion for many birders is keeping a lifer list—a list of birds they have sighted and identified over the years.

Students can start their own lifer lists, beginning with the birds in the schoolyard and in the backyards of their homes. Avid birders from the community can lead birding expeditions to nearby areas and share their knowledge about birds and birdwatching skills. Skilled birdwatchers can teach students how to identify a bird by its sound, its silhouette, or a single striking marking.

Students can draw pictures of the birds they identify and create local bird guides to the schoolyard habitat or their own backyards.

With identification of local birds as the starting point, students can progress to learning about bird anatomy and how birds are peculiarly adapted for flight. They can study flight patterns and migration habits.

The Working Landscape: Local Resource-Based Industries

Students can learn about the working landscape by talking to community members who work on the land to make a living and meet local needs.

Have the students draw up a list of local industries that rely on or make direct use of natural resources, such as:

farming

sugaring

hunting, fishing, trapping

logging

milling (grist, saw)

mining (granite, slate, copper)

generating hydroelectric power

Invite individuals to the classroom who work in these industries and have students interview them. For example, a logger could describe how he cuts down trees and what equipment he uses. A sawmill operator could explain how logs are processed into lumber and plywood.

Forestry

Invite a local forester to the classroom and have students interview him or her. Following are some suggested questions to ask.

- What was the forest like before European settlers arrived? What impact did the native population have on the forest?
- Why did the settlers initially clear the land? How did they clear it?
- How did clearing the land impact the animals? the soil? the climate?
- What are the stages of forest growth? How does the forest reseed itself?
- How do foresters help sustain our forests? Has this changed? How? Why or why not?

Arrange to go on a walking tour with a local forester of a nearby wooded area. Foresters can impart much knowledge to students even if the walk takes place in nothing more exotic than a small park in town. They are skilled in identifying trees and can note the succession stage, and they can point out potential problems, such as signs of disease, insect damage, and pollution.

Traditional Crafts: Making Local History

An excellent way for students to connect with elders is to invite them to the class to share some of the household crafts that they learned from their childhood, practical arts that met the real needs of a household as part of an agrarian tradition.

Imagine if we were able to harvest the talent of our community and pass it on—how rich our children would be! Not only would they learn the skills of making these age-old crafts, but they would be building new friendships in the same way that these elderly people learned the crafts themselves.

For example, Libby, an eighty-plus member of the Peacham, Vermont community, was delighted to come into the local school and teach the children how to make balsam bags. She sat among the children and told them that this is something she learned from her mother as a child. She used to put them under her pillow, she said, as well as in her closets and drawers, as a fragrance.

After listening intently to her story, each child pulled balsam needles off the dried branches and eagerly began filling bags to make their very own. The Peacham teachers later reported that many of those same students kept those bags in their school locker for the entire year and said that they thought of Libby every time they pulled their bags out. The bags and the making of them now had meaning, a larger context.

This little story illustrates a way to preserve a local craft, passed down over the generations and now in danger of being forgotten. But by reconnecting students and elder craftspeople, students can, through hands-on demonstration, learn and thereby preserve these skills.

Sample Craft Projects with Area Elders

- Basket weaving
- Barrel making
- Book making
- Candle making
- Canoe making
- Chair caning
- Lathing
- Leather crafts
- Musical instruments
- Needlepoint
- Painting
- Quilting
- Rail splitting
- Sewing and knitting
- Shingle making
- Snowshoe making
- Soap making
- Stenciling
- Tanning
- Weaving
- Whittling

Directions for Making Local History Through Crafts

1. **Selection of Craftsperson.** Survey local craftspeople and artisans. Working through a parent or community liaison, find out who would be willing to share his or her skill with children.

2. **Curriculum Integration.** Design a curriculum unit around local history and the role of crafts and arts in preserving local culture; draw on learning standards in language arts, history, science, math, and the creative arts.

3. **Scheduling.** Create a schedule (weekly, biweekly or monthly) for working with a local guest who can come and lead students in making a craft. Parents and other community members can also be involved by working with small groups of students.

An excellent way for students to connect with elders is to invite them to the class to share some of the household crafts that they learned from their childhood, practical arts that met the real needs of a family as part of an agrarian tradition.

4. **Documentation and Assessment.** Conduct a KWL with each student: Find out what they already *Know*; discover what they *Want* to know; and at the end of the project, find out what they *Learned*. Document each step of the process through portfolios, photographs, and video.

5. **Presentation and Performance.** Have students explain the history of the craft, how this person came to learn it, its role in the culture, how it was made, what it was used for. This can become a book of local crafts.

BAG IT!
Making Balsam Bags

Standard(s) Being Addressed

1.18	Information Technology	4.5	Continuity and Change
1.19	Research	6.6	Being a Historian
3.10	Teamwork	6.8	Movements and Settlements
4.1	Service	7.1	Scientific Method
7.7	Measurement		

Inquiry/Focusing Questions

Where did people get the materials they needed to make and build things?

What hobbies were common among the people living in our community a century ago, and why?

What crafts did the children of our community make that are still being made by children today? Which ones are no longer made and why?

What were all the ways in which our community ancestors used trees?

How does the way we use and value nature compare to the way our community ancestors used and valued nature?

Topic

Learning traditional crafts, resourcefulness and the value of nature, the skill of being a historian, and the value and wisdom of our elders

Materials

blank graph paper
needles and thread, rulers (tape measures), scissors
cloth and yarn, balsam (balsam fir branches)
interview log books (composition booklets work well)

Procedure

1. Preassess students individually on what they know about crafts and the environment (natural resources) by asking them to map on graph paper their favorite room in their house and on the map locate (draw) as many household objects they can find that they believe are made of resources that come from the environment.
2. Divide students into heterogeneous groups based on preassessment results (encourage cooperative learning skills and division of labor). (*Note:* Each child in each group

could make his or her own bag, or groups could make a group bag or set of bags by having each member complete one part of the process, or have each group be responsible for one part of the process as they contribute toward making one whole-class bag.)

3. Explain to students that community elders will be visiting to work with them on how to make a traditional craft called the balsam bag and that their task will be to listen, observe, and help each other learn the process for when they make balsam bags for upcoming community service projects. In addition, encourage students to practice their interviewing skills by asking the elders about additional nature crafts that they can incorporate into subsequent community service projects.
4. Arrange to have someone present on the day of the event to videotape and take photographs of the students and elders working together. (*Note*: The teacher might want to videotape or tape-record the elders' lessons to replay for the students later. Older students can be asked to record observations and additional craft ideas in their interview logs while working with the elders.)
5. Invite community elders to spend time working with the students on making balsam bags.
6. Set aside time for students and elders to share their creations with one another and discuss their thoughts and feelings about the experience.
7. Arrange to have the balsam bags and a photo essay of the event prominently displayed somewhere in the community.
8. Engage students in a discussion on the activity's focusing questions.
9. Assess students' acquisition of knowledge and skills and progress toward attaining the standards being addressed.
10. Ask students to research a traditional craft of their choice, learn its origins and how to make it, and be prepared to share their knowledge with their mentoring elders.
11. Schedule follow-up sessions for students and elders to work together teaching one another their favorite traditional crafts.
12. Schedule community service projects for the students to apply their skills (crafts) in a way that serves their community.

Task-Specific Assessment

(products, performances, tasks, tools [rubrics/checklists], anecdotal observations)

pre- and postgraph paper maps — interview logs — video recording (performance)

balsam bags (products) — photo essay — research report

anecdotal observations of teamwork and time spent working with elders

Generalized Standard Assessment

1.19 Research rubric — 4.1 Service checklist

STEP 6

Community Service-Learning

Once students have confidence in the skills they have learned through the local projects they have undertaken, they will be eager to use their newfound learning to help make their community a better place. Young people have big hearts. They care about the well-being of others. When given opportunities for service-learning, they invariably leap to the challenge and want to excel showing compassion toward others.

Service-learning has come of age as a way to reconnect students to the communities in which they live. This is especially true around the holidays when food drives are commonplace in schools and the spirit of volunteerism is strong.

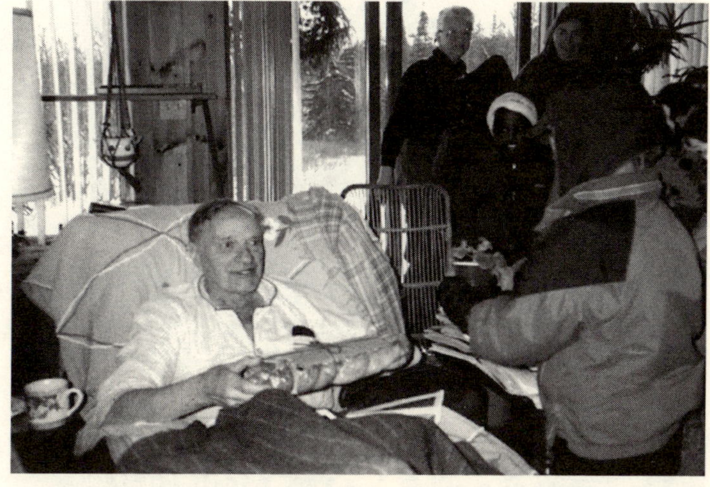

The greater aim of any holiday service-learning project, however, is to fully integrate these initiatives into the existing curriculum throughout the school year. Following is a simple process for making local service-learning projects the centerpiece of an interdisciplinary curriculum.

Six Steps for Service-Learning

Step 1: Needs Assessment

To maximize the learning experience as well as the effectiveness of the service provided, it is essential to begin with a thorough needs assessment to identify the most urgent needs of elders and other community members.

Step 2: Developing a Schoolwide Framework

After identifying the most pressing needs, design a schoolwide framework to meet those needs. A community needs assessment may reveal that large numbers of local people run out of food at the end of every month, for example. In response, the class may choose to adopt a local food pantry or soup kitchen as the focus of its service-learning curriculum and make the study of food and agricultural history part of its yearlong interdisciplinary study.

Step 3: Designing Age-Appropriate Projects

Determine service-learning initiatives appropriate to the grade levels and abilities of the students. Kindergartners and first graders, for example, would be more enthusiastic about going to a senior center or soup kitchen to sing songs and share stories than to prepare and serve meals. A group of second graders could form hospitality teams to make place mats and set tables each week at the soup kitchen, while older students could grow and cook foods out of their own gardens using recipes that they collect and test themselves. (See the Local History Framework on page 9.)

Step 4: Service-Learning Curriculum

Infuse service throughout the curriculum as part of a thematic unit. In this way, service becomes an essential part of the school philosophy and mission.

As part of a yearlong social studies theme of state history, for instance, fourth grade students could address the ongoing food and nutrition needs of local elders. First, the class could visit the statewide food bank or a regional or local emergency food shelf to see for themselves where people go who need emergency food.

For this activity, students would prepare a list of questions to ask before their visit, such as: How many people does the food bank serve per month? What kinds of food does it provide? Why do people come here? How many days' allotment of food does it provide? What are the ages and family sizes of the people who come here? What time of month is demand for food the greatest (first week, second week, third week, fourth week)? What kinds of foods does the bank tend to run out of at the end of every month, and what does it need on a monthly basis?

After addressing immediate food needs, students can then choose to focus on one specific food need that they would like to help meet, such as fresh breads and produce. An example of an ongoing service-learning project could include researching local bread recipes and making end-of-the-month donations of fresh breads with special labels listing the name of the person who contributed the bread recipe along with the ingredients.

The class could design and publish their own monthly recipe book that includes interviews of various elders along with the history of the recipes—where they came from, who passed them down, the seasonal significance of the meals, where the ingredients come from, their nutritional value, and so on. Through the process, the students would need to experiment with the recipes to determine if they would suit the tastes of the clients. It is easy to see how this service-learning initiative crosses many areas of the curriculum including social studies (research, oral history), language arts (research, writing reports, recipes, ongoing documentation), science (recipes, botany, nutrition), math (determining monthly food needs, recipe experimentation), art (bread labels, recipe book with drawings), and technology (scanning photographs, using digital cameras to photograph the process, presenting a slide show).

Step 5: Assessment and Documentation

The inclusion of ongoing assessments into individual student portfolios will help to tell a more complete story of what has been learned. These assessment portfolios could include evidence of students' prior knowledge, the activities they undertook, the standards addressed and rubrics used, students' self-assessments and affective surveys, plus documentation through photographs, video, creative arts, cooking, baking, and crafts. Creative arts provide tangible evidence that students have obtained specific learning standards. Ongoing assessments will also clearly reveal students' feelings about the service-learning activities they have undertaken.

Step 6: Recycling

From examining the process and results of service-learning in Steps 1 through 5, students and teachers can then determine the next stage of their work, the next level of service-learning that they would like to embark on. What worked? What didn't? What are the highest needs? How can we address those needs given what we have learned?

Extracurricular field trips, such as to food banks, are an excellent way to begin a community service-learning curriculum in the school by demonstrating the potential applications for applied learning.

Teachers can devise other service-learning projects that can be used to develop an integrated curriculum. A service-learning methodology shows how acts of compassion can cross an interdisciplinary thematic curriculum and be an ongoing way of maintaining the connection between home, school, and community. The ideal is to cross all the disciplines as part of an integrated way of learning.

HUNGRY TO LEARN
Adopting a Local Food Shelf

Standard(s) Being Addressed

- 2.2 Problem Solving
- 3.10 Teamwork
- 7.9 Statistics and Probability Concepts
- 4.1 Service
- 7.1 Scientific Method

Inquiry/Focusing Questions

What happens to our bodies when we don't eat?

What are the differences between hunger, malnutrition, and starvation?

Did our community ancestors ever suffer from hunger, malnutrition, or starvation? If so, why?

Do any community members suffer from frequent hunger or malnutrition? If so, why?

What are the essential foods people need to avoid malnutrition or starvation?

Is there anything we can do to make sure no one in our community suffers from hunger or malnutrition?

Topic

Learning about hunger and the economics of food, and cultivating a community service ethic

Materials

social service agency reference materials

graph paper and markers

student- and elder-produced foods or meals

food packaging and storage materials

transportation

blank KWL forms

Procedures

1. Preassess students individually using a KWL form to determine what students know about hunger, malnutrition, starvation, and famine.

2. Divide students into heterogeneous groups (encourage cooperative learning skills and division of labor).
3. Ask students to develop a set of interview questions to ask their mentoring elders regarding the elders' knowledge of and experiences with past and present hunger in the community.
4. Invite mentoring elders to be interviewed by the students. (*Note:* Remind elders of confidentiality issues to be sure they don't mention people's names.)
5. Ask students and their mentoring elders to research the reference materials for relevant statistics such as number of local families receiving public assistance, number of people using local food shelves and soup kitchens, local health statistics, etc., and to create graphs, tables, or pie charts representing these data over time.
6. Ask students to present their findings and conclusions and to share their proposals on how their ongoing "Baking with Elders" program can help people needing assistance.
7. Engage students and elders in a discussion on how the elders' experience with local hunger (qualitative data) compares or contrasts with the quantitative data contained in the reference materials.
8. Ask your community coordinator(s) to make arrangements with a local food shelf or soup kitchen to form a partnership with the students and elders and to coordinate transportation of food, students, and elders to and from the food shelf or soup kitchen.
9. Engage students in a discussion on the activity's focusing questions.
10. Assess students' acquisition of knowledge and skills and progress toward attaining the standards being addressed.
11. Arrange for the students and elders to visit the local food shelf or soup kitchen they've adopted as a partner in their fight against local hunger.

Task-Specific Assessment

(products, performances, tasks, tools [rubrics/checklists], anecdotal observations)

pre- and post-KWLs — data presentations
interview questions — foods or meals (products)
anecdotal observations of teamwork, discussion time, and time with elders

Generalized-Standard Assessment

4.1 Service Checklist — 7.9 Statistics and Probability rubric

FROM VERMONT

Garden of Change

Food for All, Serve and Learn

Kindergarten teacher Roni Donnenfeld at the Warren School in central Vermont has developed a year-round integrated curriculum organized around gardening and preparing food that covers all the major subject areas through a service-learning project.

Several years ago Roni and her students decided to build a kiva garden at the entrance to the school. Students, working together with their families, hauled stones from the nearby woods and built a circular fieldstone courtyard surrounded by wooden container gardens complete with arbors as entranceways.

Alongside the garden, local flatbread baker George Schenk worked with the students to build an outdoor beehive-style bread oven made of brick and clay, reflecting traditional New England and Quebec designs of the seventeenth and eighteenth centuries.

Roni and her students call their garden the "Garden of Change." The class decided to grow the vegetables needed to make tomato sauce, which they spread on the bread they bake in their oven. They then donate their special "Kindergarten Flatbreads" to the community.

Of the one hundred flatbreads Roni's class makes yearly, many are served at the community's fall harvest supper, more are given to local families in need, some are donated to the pediatric ward at a nearby hospital, others are given to a battered women's shelter, and the rest students take home to their families.

Using gardening, bread making, and community service as her organizing principle, Roni has built an entire curriculum around the class's garden. For science, students draw pictures of flowers, leaves, and tomatoes, record their initial observations, and predict how the plants will change in the weeks to come. The children model the scientific method by recording, in their own words and pictures, the changes they observe over time and revising their predictions accordingly.

For social studies, students learn the history of cultivating and preparing food in their immediate community and wider region, as well as how people have helped one another by sharing bread, produce, and other foods.

For math studies, students calculate how much sauce they need for one hundred flatbreads—how many tomatoes and onions, how much garlic and olive oil. They discover how long it takes to bake a flatbread in a 500-degree oven and how long it takes to bake one hundred loaves.

For language arts, children learn a whole new vocabulary for gardening, plants, bread making, food preparation, and building. They dictate and record in their journals their ongoing observations and practice their communication, listening, speaking, and problem-solving skills in deciding what to grow, how to cultivate and harvest, how to prepare the harvest, and who to give the flatbreads based on need.

Roni's garden project is just one example of how service-learning can become the founding philosophy of a teacher's pedagogy, making student learning across the disciplines blend in seamlessly with service to the wider community.

Roni's garden project is just one example of how service-learning can become the founding philosophy of a teacher's pedagogy, making student learning across the disciplines blend in seamlessly with service to the wider community.

Step 7

Culminating Celebration

Planning, at the outset of a local history project, to hold a community wide culminating activity motivates students by providing a framework for identifying clear goals to work toward. Knowing the culminating activity from the start also spells out the project expectations to the students, teachers, parents, and community members who will be taking part in the celebration.

Like choosing a mountain to climb, having a culminating celebration as a fixed goal at the beginning of the journey serves to direct the group's energy toward a shared purpose. There will be ample opportunity during the hike to look back and appreciate the view and the work that's been done to reach each plateau. Experienced hikers recognize that each step is a lesson in itself—an opportunity to absorb the sounds and sights, the mystery of the journey. And throughout their journey they know that, beyond this summit, there are still more mountains to climb.

Following the Ancient Cycle of the Seasons

When the place-based curriculum is envisioned as a yearlong initiative, there will naturally be seasonal celebrations that serve as regular culminating activities throughout the year. Some of these can neatly coincide with holidays from our own cultural calendar, such as Thanksgiving. Other celebrations can coincide with the fall and spring equinoxes or the winter solstice or tie in with the local agrarian culture, such as a spring planting festival. These festivals provide an opportunity to honor and realign with our collective agrarian heritage, which values the natural world as the foundation for our cultural and intellectual lives.

Indigenous cultures throughout the world can teach us that all nature should be respected and held sacred. They took nothing for granted; all signs in nature were understood as a teaching, a lesson on the journey. Native peoples respected the elders for all that they had learned and experienced and as living representatives of the ancestors who watched over and protected them.

Growing out of this intimate relationship with nature was a reverence and gratitude that culminated in ceremonies where people sang, danced, and ate the food that had been gathered or grown and harvested together. In Native American traditions, these celebrations are sacred occasions to give thanks that the group made it through another season, that the earth provided once again, and that nature always prevails.

Community wide seasonal gatherings allow students to become more aware of and experience the natural cycles that have shaped human settlements from the outset and define who we are. This is the intergenerational learning that local history projects can promote.

The opening ceremony for a school's earth garden. Each raised bed is in the shape of one of the continents.

Music celebration and celebration of community and place at Meek High School in Arley, Alabama. Photo courtesy Program for Rural Services and Research.

Planning for Culminating Seasonal Activities

1. Intentionally plan the yearlong study, seasonal units, and culminating seasonal activities. Fine-tune and clarify each seasonal unit by thinking ahead to those culminating events.
2. Drawing from local history, plan each seasonal culminating activity to coincide with traditional events. If local history is the theme, find dates of local events or celebrations when people usually come together.
3. Create task-specific checklists so students know what is expected of them in advance of the culminating activity.

Preparing for and Presenting the Culminating Seasonal Activity

Preparation

1. Have the students individually invite all elders and community members whom they interviewed or worked with in any way to the event.
2. Post and distribute fliers inviting all parents and community members to attend.
3. Send press releases inviting the local press to attend and document this important demonstration of student and community learning.
4. Organize student rehearsal and prepare displays. Use music, song, and poetry to present what students learned from elders. Their presentations should reflect what they learned from elders about their local history and could include posters, displays, dioramas, artifacts, photos, slides, collages, written materials, skits, and big books.
5. Plan what food will be served.

Presentation

1. Students make presentations, either individually or in small groups, following their checklist of what was expected.
2. After students have made their presentations, they invite the elders who were their mentors to stand for community applause to honor the passing down of their traditional knowledge.
3. Allow time toward the end of the formal program for people to mingle at student displays and ask questions.

Assessment

Conduct student, teacher, and community assessments of the culminating activity and begin to plan for the next seasonal cycle.

INSTANT REPLAY
Reenacting Local History

Standard(s) Being Addressed

1.18	Information Technology	4.5	Continuity and Change
1.19	Research	6.6	Being a Historian
2.2	Problem Solving	6.8	Movements and Settlements
3.10	Teamwork		

Inquiry/Focusing Questions

What was life like during the early days of our community?

What major historical events took place where we now live?

Of all the events that have taken place over time in our community, which one had the most impact on our local culture? on our local environment?

Of all the events that have taken place over time in our community, which one had the most impact on you?

If you could go back in time, during which period of our local history would you choose to live? Why?

What does history tell us about the connection between the natural heritage and cultural heritage of our community?

Topic

Honoring the local community and its cultural heritage through reenacting local history

Materials

local history reference materials

variety of art/construction media (papier-mâché, tissue paper, clay, Play-Doh, cardboard, construction paper, scissors, paint, brushes) for costumes

props and backdrop

musical instruments

video recorder

student- and elder-prepared traditional snacks for after the show

blank timelines

community feedback forms

Procedure

1. Schedule a time for the students to present their upcoming reenactments and begin advertising (posters, fliers) and inviting the community to attend this special event.
2. Preassess students individually using a blank or partially completed timeline to find out what they know about local history.
3. Divide students into heterogeneous groups (encourage cooperative learning skills and division of labor). (*Note:* Each group could reenact a different local historical event, or each could develop one part of a whole-class reenactment.)
4. Ask students to review the reference materials and come to a consensus on which local historical event(s) they would like to reenact.
5. Provide students with time to research their event(s) of choice.
6. Ask students to supplement their research by developing a set of interview questions to ask their mentoring elders regarding the historical event(s) they've chosen to reenact.
7. Invite the elders to interview with the students.
8. Ask students and elders to discuss how the elders' recollections of the event(s) compare or contrast with what's stated in the reference materials.
9. Provide students and mentoring elders time to produce and practice their reenactments. Remind students that the purpose of a culminating activity is that it provides them with an opportunity to comprehensively demonstrate the knowledge and skills they've acquired throughout the entire unit and that they will want to include as much of what they've learned in their reenactment as possible.
10. Performance day/culminating activity! Provide audience with feedback forms to help assess students' work. Don't forget to videotape the event, and don't forget the traditional snacks afterward.
11. Engage students in a follow-up discussion on the activity's focusing questions.
12. Assess students' acquisition of knowledge and progress toward attaining the standards being addressed.
13. Celebrate the students' work with a special viewing of the video.

Task-Specific Assessment

(products, performances, tasks, tools [rubrics/checklists], anecdotal observations)

pre- and post-timelines
costumes, props, and backdrop (products)
community feedback forms
anecdotal observations of teamwork and discussion times
reenactment and/or video (performance)
interviews/interview questions

Generalized-Standard Assessment

Any and/or all of the generalized, embedded standards rubrics/checklists

FROM CALIFORNIA

California Oral History

Students Record Voices of the Valley

Seventh- through twelfth-grade students in Anderson Valley, in the redwoods and wine-growing region of Mendocino County in Northern California, have joined the ranks of community historians by producing annual books and compact discs that collect and preserve the stories of their elders. Titled *Voices of the Valley*, the project connects young people with the older citizens of Anderson Valley, in the process giving them an important link to their community's past, as well as giving the elders a new appreciation of the talents that their community's youth possess.

What started as an effort by eight junior high students in 1997, has blossomed into an established course in the ninth- to twelfth-grade curriculum. Last spring, volumes I and II were honored at the Library of Congress in Washington, D.C., as a Local Legacies Project, celebrating the bicentennial of the nation's library.

Each staff of student historians designs the scope and sequence of each volume of *Voices of the Valley*. The project's creator, Mitch Mendosa, who is also the Anderson Valley Coordinator of the North Coast Rural Challenge Network, points out that the students must own the project for it to have any real meaning to them. To that end, students take charge of every aspect of the work, including creating the focus of each volume, contacting the elders to set up preinterview and interview sessions, improving their communicative skills, mastering digital audio recording, editing, and CD production, digital photography editing, the seemingly endless hours of word processing, book layout, and advertising and sales.

Each staff of student historians learns lessons that aren't traditionally covered in classrooms. The economic base in Anderson Valley has shifted, for example, from logging, sheep ranching, and apple farming to grape growing for wine production and a few small businesses. The cultural makeup of the Valley has also changed dramatically during the last two decades. Interviewing elders who represented these different groups gives students an accurate representation of Anderson Valley life both past and present, seeing what has changed and what has stayed the same while acknowledging and celebrating those differences. The hundreds of people who have read and listened to their work have gained this knowledge as well.

Not just writing down but preserving the actual voices of the elders is a priority of *Voices of the Valley*. Each book has an accompanying compact disc that includes interview excerpts linked by music from local performers and student musicians.

Sadly, in the course of completing the inter-

views, four of the elders interviewed have died. Though each death stuns the students, they also gain a poignant understanding of the importance of their endeavor.

"It meant a lot for the youth of Anderson Valley to be at the funerals," Oral History Project student Nicole Breit commented. "We were pretty much the only young people there who knew these older people."

Kelsy Harnist added, "The death of some of the people we interviewed made me realize that it's important for us to get to know older people outside of the project because they may not be around for much longer and their incredible stories will be lost."

Mendosa commented, "As an educator, I've found it extremely valuable to involve students in the process of collecting our community's stories. Our children are far too removed from the people around them. The numerous distractions that our youth are exposed to make it very difficult for them to gain a true sense of the diversity and history of their communities. Also, we spend a great deal of time focusing on historical events in places far away. and too often miss the richness of what's in our own backyard.

"Enabling students to go out into their communities with the important task of collecting and preserving local history connects them with their neighbors in a meaningful way. The students and I come away from each interview with a sense that something special has just occurred and that learning has taken on new meaning. This, in my mind, is one of the most powerful educational experiences we can offer our students."

Adapted from Rural Matters, *Fall 1999. To purchase a book and CD, call Mitch Mendosa at (707) 895-2199 or e-mail at <mmendosa@avusd.k12.ca.us>.*

STEP 8

Assessing and Evaluating

This section describes the step-by-step process that classroom teachers can use to regularly assess and evaluate the impact of their local history program on their students and the community-at-large. The information provided in this section can be used to help organize and implement a comprehensive plan for assessing and evaluating the overall effectiveness of a local history curriculum, particularly student progress toward meeting identified educational standards and goals being addressed, as well as the program's impact on the wider community.

By implementing this process over the course of their local history curricula, teachers will have successfully answered three key questions for assessing and evaluating the impact of their ongoing local history study.

1. What learning standards and goals will students attain through this course of study and how will that be assessed and documented?

2. How can students use their research and documentation to better tell the story of the people, places and events in their community's history?

3. How can the study of local history by students meet the current needs of the community and enhance its unique identity and sense of pride?

The design and implementation of a purposeful assessment and evaluation plan obviously requires additional time and effort. The short- and long-term benefits gained by the teachers, students, and community members as a result of this effort make that time well worth the investment.

In the following pages, the purpose of assessment and evaluation is discussed, along with the differences between the two and the benefits both provide. A bread-making assessment activity is provided as an example of using a local history lesson as two activities (instruction and assessment) in one.

We conclude the chapter by taking a look at tools for developing an overall program assessment and evaluation plan—beginning with student assessment—and the importance of implementing such a plan. Based on the comprehensive assessment conducted over the course of the unit, an authoritative and well-documented evaluation can be completed using the evaluation forms provided at the end of the chapter.

Why Assess and Evaluate?

Administrators and educators must justify their work with concrete data and results that show the effectiveness of their curriculum choices. Without reliable evidence and statistics, they are left only with anecdotal observations, which, alone, policy makers rarely accept as sufficient evidence.

An ongoing, rigorous assessment plan will help teachers document the impact of explorations into the history of the community on young learners. If teachers can show how they have met the goals outlined in their school's curriculum plan, they will have a powerful local model to encourage other teachers to integrate local history into their curricula. In addition, teachers will be able to provide their community with evidence that their school's local history program has a lasting effect on the lives of their children. With assessment and evaluation results in hand, teachers have the perfect entrée for demonstrating to school boards, administrators, and community members why local history curricula should become a major focus for every school. This is a bridge for connecting schools to the heart of their community; a rationale explaining how children learn by exploring their heritage and why it is essential to integrate local history into the school's curriculum.

Assessing and evaluating the worth of a local history curriculum is no simple task. For any teacher, the challenge of organizing, planning, and conducting local history research in an educational environment increasingly fixated on more global technology and perspectives is an ambitious undertaking. Added to this is the practical need to assess each step of the process to justify its academic relevance.

If documentation tools are put into place from the beginning, however, and regularly integrated into the program on an ongoing basis, teachers will be left with a plethora of supporting data. For example, teachers can use creative arts activities to enhance and highlight the study, collecting samples of students' artwork as well as recording their reactions to specific activities in the students' journals. Both the artwork and their responses are forms of documentation that can be used to assess and ultimately evaluate the curriculum.

Although it may seem obvious that understanding one's own community is crucial for nurturing the whole child, anecdotal evidence of this, alone, is not enough to convince the wider community of its effectiveness. To justify an ongoing local history study, teachers need a combination of qualitative and quantitative evidence. Stories, samples of student work, newspaper clippings, and visual documentation, such as photographs and video, are just a few examples of qualitative evidence that can be used in conjunction with quantitative data obtained through evaluation.

The Assessment and Evaluation Process

Assessment and evaluation are not the same, yet the words are often used interchangeably. Assessment is a qualitative monitoring of process. It assists students or programs in meeting specific criteria and prepares them to succeed when it comes time for final evaluation. Evaluation is a quantitative categorizing of product. The purpose of assessment is to guide. The purpose of evaluation is to grade.

Assessing and Evaluating Student Progress and Performance

Student Assessment

Assessment involves monitoring student performance over time. It is the ongoing gathering of information on student progress. Evaluation entails placing a value on a specific project, product, or performance once completed.

Assessment is intended to provide an opportunity to monitor how well the student is progressing toward specific expectations or outcomes. Assessment should be informative, direct instruction or implementation and ultimately prepare a student for success at final evaluation time. Assessment is not the end in itself, but rather a means of achieving an end.

Assessment Tools

The three basic forms of assessment are: activities, tasks, and tools (scoring guides). These assessments are used differently, yet all serve the same purpose of helping to gather information on a student's progress.

An assessment activity is any classroom lesson or activity that engages students in a way that allows the teacher to instruct and assess simultaneously. A sample of an assessment activity is described below.

Assessment tasks are informal measures that are deliberately designed for checking in to see how well students are progressing. Typical assessment tasks include journal entries, conferences, surveys, and graphic organizers, such as Venn diagrams, concept webs, and KWLs.

Assessment tools (scoring guides) are formal measures against which a student's progress is compared. Rubrics and checklists are two standard assessment tools. In both cases, specific criteria (expected outcomes/indicators of success) are listed within a continuum that reflects where the student stands in terms of progress toward those expected outcomes.

Program Goals

One of the goals of teaching local history is to encourage children to develop a healthy respect for and appreciation of their community. With this goal in mind, the teacher can now design a culminating activity (for example, a community heritage celebration with students exhibiting and discussing their final projects) and series of enabling activities, such as the bread-making activity on page 122, which together will help students achieve those goals.

Keeping clear goals in mind also allows the teacher to plan what assessment tasks and tools will be used so that the teacher and students can monitor how well the students are progressing toward meeting those goals. Tasks will include pre-, midpoint, and postassessments that might include affective surveys measuring students' attitudes, journal entries, and graphic organizers, such as concept webs measuring students' acquisition of knowledge. Tools (scoring guides) will include the more formal rubrics or checklists the teacher has designed. These periodic, criteria-based assessments not only monitor progress and direct instruction, but also reinforce the knowledge, skills, and attitudes students are developing. All these assessments are collected and maintained in the students' individual portfolios. Student portfolios are co-maintained by the teacher and students and are accessible to students anytime, enabling them to monitor their progress in meeting the goals of the program on an ongoing basis.

Student Evaluation

Once students have been given multiple opportunities (through various assessment activities, tasks, and tools) to develop the knowledge, skills, and attitudes expected of them, they are then ready to be evaluated in those areas. Final evaluation measuring students' overall progress entails quantifying the various assessments that have been collected and maintained in the students' portfolios. To quantify student progress, the teacher creates a checklist of desired outcomes that align with the knowledge and skills regularly being assessed and tabulates the number of those outcomes met as evidenced by the student's assessment results. The final evaluation objectively quantifies

Bread Making: A Sample Assessment Activity

Instructing students on the historical value of bread, then allowing them to make, bake, and eat their own heritage breads, can help promote in students a sense of pride in their local history and cultural heritage. Bread making is not only an effective enabling activity but also can serve as an assessment activity as well.

For example, before beginning the lesson, the teacher might first conduct a preassessment that gauges students' knowledge and attitudes about bread making in their community. The teacher could ask students to describe how they think bread has been made throughout history, or ask them to draw a picture showing how bread was made one hundred or more years ago and compare that with a drawing of how bread is made today. These preassessments will reveal much about students' existing knowledge and prior experiences, which, in turn, will help direct the teacher's instruction.

Once the preassessment is completed, students can then begin to learn how bread has been made in the past. During instruction and class discussion, ongoing assessment can be conducted by relating questions to students' preassessed knowledge and noting their responses.

After providing students with necessary background information (some of which will have been determined by the preassessment results), students are then ready to conduct research by interviewing community members and learning about bread-making techniques and equipment used in the past. As they are participating in this process, the teacher can again listen to their conversations, observe their behavior and level of participation, and record these observations in an anecdotal observation log. A midpoint assessment might also be conducted to determine whether or not students' interest in bread making is changing now that they are more personally involved with the process.

After the students have researched, baked, and eaten breads from the past, a postassessment can then be conducted. For a direct before-and-after comparison, students can be given the same task they were given as a preassessment. Each of the two preassessment tasks described earlier would serve well for comparing before-and-after snapshots of the students' knowledge and attitudes.

A second way to integrate assessment and instruction is to design activities that are actually students' progress and reflects whether or not they have met the specific criteria that were the focus of ongoing instruction and assessment.

Evaluation involves assigning value to a final product or performance. Unlike assessment, evaluation is quantitative and serves as an end in itself. Typically, a product or performance is given a letter grade, a numerical grade, or placed in a percentile that reflects the number of predetermined criteria the product or performance has met. Evaluation can be more objective than assessment provided the criteria for evaluation are clearly stated beforehand and extensively taught, reinforced, and assessed. Continuous assessment informs students of their progress in those particular areas and informs teachers how to better assist students in meeting their goals. In other words, ongoing assessment helps prepare students to succeed in their final evaluation.

assessments themselves. Problem-solving activities in which students must apply knowledge and skills previously learned while at the same time learn new information are excellent examples of activities that allow for simultaneous instruction and assessment.

For example, once students have learned different bread-making techniques, teams of students might each be given a recipe collected from the community. In attempting to gather the ingredients and bake their particular bread, students are challenged to deduce the history of the bread based on where the ingredients come from, the equipment needed to produce the ingredients, and the equipment needed to successfully bake the bread. Alternatively, students can experiment with various ingredients and develop new bread recipes. In both cases, students will learn additional information about the process of bread making and be assessed on how well they remember and apply what they previously learned.

Assessment informs teachers on how well they're doing, what is and isn't working, and what steps need to be taken next. If teachers assess as they go along, not only are they able to accumulate information about their students, they are also able to monitor the effectiveness of their individual activities and their program as a whole. They are more informed, their instruction improves, and the effectiveness and success of their programs are enhanced.

ASSESSING AND EVALUATING THE OVERALL PROGRAM

Program Assessment

Assessing an overall program is a task broader than assessing student performance. Student performance is just of one of several elements critical to assessing and evaluating the overall effectiveness of a local history program. Other elements include the students' general affect, teacher anecdotes and reflections, and the community's general response and participation.

Developing and maintaining an ongoing program assessment portfolio similar to the student portfolio described above is an effective method of assessing the success of an overall program. Program portfolios, like student portfolios, should contain a comprehensive collection of products, performance artifacts, tasks, tools (scoring guides), and anecdotal evidence that will ultimately tell the story of the program and its effectiveness. Contents might include: student portfolios, student affective surveys (if not already part of their portfolios), teacher reflection logs, community attendance records, community surveys, classroom participant surveys, a school-community scrapbook (a collection of fliers, press releases, newspaper articles, photographs, memorable quotes, thank-you notes, letters), and culminating activity surveys completed by community attendees.

Program Evaluation

As stated earlier, evaluation is objective quantification of qualitative assessment results. To quantify a program's success, the teacher must first determine a set of desired outcomes (criteria) that align with the criteria that are regularly being assessed throughout the program. For our local history program, the criteria regularly being assessed include student performance, student affect, teacher affect, and community response. Therefore, a corresponding final evaluation checklist might read:

FINAL PROGRAM EVALUATION CHECKLIST

___ Students' portfolios (products, performance artifacts, tasks, tools [scoring guides], anecdotal observations, and self-assessments) collectively show progress in acquisition of knowledge and skills.

___ Students' portfolios collectively show proficiency in application of knowledge and skills acquired.

___ Students' affective surveys collectively reveal a consistently positive response to the program.

___ Teacher's reflections reveal an overall positive feeling about the program.

___ Community attendance records indicate sustained or increased participation over the course of the program.

___ Community surveys collectively reveal a consistently positive response to the program.

___ Classroom participant (community member) surveys collectively reveal a consistently positive response to the program.

___ Culminating activity surveys collectively reveal a positive response to the program.

___ School-community scrapbook reveals an overall positive response to the program.

Those evaluating the program might decide to use the percentage of criteria checked as the final rating of the program's success, or they might decide that for the program to be considered a success, each criterion on the checklist must be met.

OVERALL PROGRAM EFFECTIVENESS

On completing the final evaluation, teachers and students are encouraged to create a narrative summary of their study of local history and the program's overall effectiveness. After reviewing all their assessment and evaluation results, teachers can begin summarizing what worked well and determining next steps by first answering the following questions.

Program Summary

1. Describe how your program met a diversity of youth interests: educational, horticultural, recreational, historical, nutritional, artistic, etc. Be sure to specify by drawing from the program portfolio and exemplars contained in your students' portfolios.

2. How effective was the program in involving the community, parents, elders, and the media through community meals, celebrations, and the arts and theater?

3. What impact did the local history program have on the self-esteem of participants? How did conducting local research and interviewing community members affect students' awareness of their local community and cultural heritage? How did working with elders and other community members influence their attitudes and behavior?

4. What unexpected surprises arose, such as an inspired sense of community pride, a new relationship, a weekly storytelling circle, a new classroom tradition, an improvisational theater troupe, or a weekly gift to a local food shelf?

Assessment and Evaluation Organizers

The following forms are ready-to-use tools to help teachers organize and implement the process described above for assessing and evaluating local history programs.

Worksheet 1: Local History Activities Matrix

A matrix for tracking weekly events, such as topics covered, student activities, time spent with elders and other community members, and learning environment.

Worksheet 2: Student Portfolio Cover Sheet

A form for tallying the products, performance artifacts, tasks, tools (scoring guides), affective surveys, self-assessments, and anecdotal notes kept as evidence of overall student learning over the course of the program.

Worksheet 3: Program Portfolio Cover Sheet

A form for tallying assessments, such as teacher reflections, community surveys, and school-community scrapbooks, kept as evidence of the overall program's effectiveness and success.

Worksheet 4: Culminating Activity Checklist

A checklist that can be used as a guide for planning instruction and designing enabling activities, a tool for assessing student progress during the course of the program, and, finally, a tool for evaluating student performance on their culminating projects.

Worksheet 5: Final Program Evaluation Checklist

See checklist on previous page.

Worksheet 6: Program Summary

See "Overall Program Effectiveness" on previous page.

Worksheet I
Local History Activity Matrix

Name ______________________ **Grade Level** __________ **Week** __________

This form documents data in a systematic way to help analyze patterns in the program and factors contributing to the success of the program. After the final program evaluation is completed, this information might help determine why particular areas of the program were or were not successful.

Activity	Number of Elders	Number of Community Guests	An In-School Activity	An Out-of-School Activity	General Sense of Success

Recommendations for next week:

Worksheet 2
STUDENT PORTFOLIO COVER SHEET

Each time one of the assessments listed is put in the student's portfolio, mark the date it was entered and keep a running tally. A good balance of documentation, featuring multiple examples of each of these forms of assessment, will provide a holistic picture of student performance and progress. At the conclusion of the program, a Student Exemplar Portfolio can be created, which would include the best pieces from each assessment category.

Assessment	Dates	Tally
Products		
Performances (or performance artifacts)		
Tasks (e.g., graphic organizers, journal entries)		
Tools (scoring guides)		
Affective Surveys		
Self-Assessments		
Peer Assessments		
Anecdotal Observations		

Important note: Video recording is an effective way to document students' products, performances, and affective evidence, which might otherwise be difficult to capture as evidence for documenting student performance and progress.

Worksheet 3
PROGRAM PORTFOLIO COVER SHEET

Each time one of the assessments listed is placed in the program portfolio, mark the date it was entered. A good balance of documentation, featuring multiple examples of each of these forms of assessment, will provide a holistic picture of your program. At the conclusion of the program, a Program Exemplar Portfolio can be created, which would include the best pieces from each assessment category.

Assessment	Dates	Tally
Student Portfolios (or individual excerpts)		
Student Affective Surveys		
Teacher Reflection Logs (or excerpts)		
Community Attendance Records		
Community Surveys		
Classroom Participant Surveys		
School-Community Scrapbook (or excerpts)		
Culminating Activity Surveys		

Important note: Video recording of the activities and events that occurred during the program is an effective way to document products, performances, and affective evidence which might otherwise be difficult to capture as evidence for documenting the effectiveness and success of your program.

Worksheet 4
Culminating Activity Checklist

Name ______________________________ **Date** __________
Activity ______________________________

A culminating activity checklist can be used as a guide for planning instruction and designing enabling activities, a tool for assessing student progress during the course of the program, and, finally, a tool for evaluating student performance on culminating projects.

_____ **Demonstrates knowledge of our community's cultural heritage.**

_____ **Demonstrates knowledge of our community's natural heritage.**

_____ **Answers the unit's essential and focusing questions.**

_____ **Demonstrates progress in or attainment of standards being addressed.**

Standards Being Assessed

_____ ______________________________

_____ ______________________________

_____ ______________________________

_____ ______________________________

_____ **Reflects student gain in expertise.**

_____ **Purpose is obvious.**

_____ **Information is clear.**

_____ **Presentation is effective and considerate of the audience.**

_____ **Effort demonstrates interest, enthusiasm, and investment.**

Final Evaluation (Percent/Grade for Culminating Project)

LOCAL JEOPARDY

Standards Being Addressed

2.2	Problem Solving	4.5	Continuity and Change
3.10	Teamwork	6.8	Movements and Settlements

Inquiry/Focusing Questions

What have I learned about my community that I can someday pass on to my own children and grandchildren?

What do I know about my community's natural heritage and local environment?

What do I know about my community's cultural heritage and local history?

What have I learned about the connections between the natural heritage and cultural heritage of my community?

What have I learned about my own connections with my community's past and present?

Topic

Honoring the local community and its unique natural and cultural heritage in a way that is fun and demonstrates the students' developing sense of place

Materials

Jeopardy game setup (game board, points, host, questions, scorekeeper)

Procedures

1. Prepare students for when game day has been scheduled.
2. Divide students into heterogeneous groups (encourage cooperative learning skills and division of labor).
3. Provide students with time to review with one another all they've learned about their past and present community.

4. Ask students to develop sets of questions and answers to be used during the game. The teacher might want to color-code the questions so that students do not answer their own questions. Encourage students to consider all the various elements of past and present cultural and natural heritage they've been exploring with their mentoring elders throughout this community-based project. Those elements include: agriculture, architecture, arts and humanities, environment, famous names, food, industry, technology, traditional crafts, watershed. (*Note:* Each group could develop questions related to all the topics explored during this unit, or each could develop questions related to just one topic explored during the unit.)
5. Invite the mentoring elders to participate on teams with the students. Perhaps the elders might prefer to fill the roles of host and scorekeeper.
6. It's Local Jeopardy time! Encourage the students to have fun and prompt them not to forget the benefits of working cooperatively.
7. Engage students in a follow-up discussion on the activity's focusing questions.
8. Assess students' acquisition of knowledge and progress toward attaining the standards being addressed.

Task-Specific Assessment

(products, performances, tasks, tools [rubrics/checklists], anecdotal observations)

student-developed questions and answers

responses to the questions

anecdotal observations of teamwork and discussion times

Generalized-Standard Assessment

3.10 Teamwork rubrics

6.8 Movements and Settlements rubric

FROM ALABAMA

The Art of History

Alabama Leads the Way Toward an Arts-Based Social Studies

The Alabama State Department of Education, among the most forward-thinking Education Departments in the United States, has decreed in their state's learning standards that the arts have intrinsic value and are worth experiencing for their own sake, providing benefits that are not available through any other means. Valuing, practicing, and knowing about the arts are fundamental to the development of students' minds and spirits. This is why, in any civilization, the arts are inseparable from the very meaning of education.

PACERS, a small schools cooperative learning project based in Tuscaloosa, facilitates community history programs in rural Alabama schools crossing the disciplines through art, music, drama, photography, graphic design, and film/video. Work done under all three of PACERS' Better Schools Building Better Communities program (Joy, Genius of Place, and Sustaining Communities) engages students in study, documentation, and celebration of their communities through the living arts.

When students write and illustrate their own literature in the Book Shows project, for example, they serve their communities as authors and illustrators. When students lay out and design the pages of their school-based community newspapers, they serve their communities as graphic designers, implementing technology in production or artwork. And when they create and perform roles based on the lives of historical figures or fictional characters, students serve their communities as dramatic artists, set designers, and playwrights.

As well as serving their community through this work, students and teachers also help their schools meet the learning goals set out by the state. Every PACERS project incorporates the history of the various arts by teaching students not only the importance and influence that the arts have had in the world, but how it ties to their community. Students learn through these projects how to create, appreciate, interpret, and analyze works of art and performances by themselves, their peers, and others.

By using an interdisciplinary approach through all the PACERS projects, schools are able to provide their students with a more balanced K–12 curriculum. Music, art, and drama are no longer just a class; they are incorporated into language arts, history, social studies, and business. The PACERS Cooperative allows schools to go beyond the written curriculum and actually teach the arts through hands-on, practical experience and work. Teachers are encouraged to transcend

Students at a Notasulga High School book show in Notasulga, Alabama. The sign in the back reads, "Book Show. Welcome to our 5th annual book display. Books are written by student authors. Every book's a winner!" Photo courtesy Program for Rural Services and Research.

traditional disciplines and grade levels to encourage students to work together and incorporate the arts into everything they do.

In these community-based history projects, students, teachers, and elders draw, write, paint, photograph, dance, sing, and act together. The learning is all evidenced through visible products—performances, publications, exhibits, and displays—that demonstrate how student learning serves to meet the state's educational goals. A list of recent student accomplishments through PACERS programs includes:

- the production of a photo magazine, *Photography: Images from Rural Places*;
- staged performances with area elders before live audiences numbering in the hundreds at both the City Stages Music Festival in Birmingham, and the Smithsonian Folklife Festival on the National Mall in Washington, D.C.;
- the production of *Elders' Wisdom, Children's Song: A Guidebook to Community Celebrations of Place*, for us by teachers, students, and community members;
- and in production is a series of books on cooperative communities featuring students' black-and-white photographs, plus a songbook for use by classroom teachers, featuring over eighty oral histories and songs written by students and elders in twenty-one rural Alabama communities.

A portable exhibit, "The Treasures of Alabama," is also near completion for display in museums, libraries, and other public spaces around the state.

It is these kinds of qualitative measures of student learning that are blazing the trail for more holistic, humanities-centered assessment and evaluation as a model for the departments of education in rural states, and for the entire country.

Adapted from the 1999 Spring Report of PACERS: Better Schools Building Better Communities. *For more information on PACERS, contact Laura Caldwell at (205) 348-6432; fax: (205) 348-2412; or address: Box 870372, Tuscaloosa, AL 35487-0372.*

PART II

Through the Seasons: Local History Throughout the Year

Cultural Literacy Unit

Fall Strand

A Sample Eight-Week Unit

Story

Our story (unit*) will be a yearlong re-creation of how our ancestors learned to live on this land and make this place their home. It will be based on the rich history and cultural heritage of our local community and begin with an exploration of our homeland's natural assets. We will get to know our land's flora, fauna, terrain, and climate. We will also become familiar with our community's place within our larger watershed. In short, we will explore the question, "Where are we?"

Once we know the natural habitats within and around our community, we will then take a trip back in time and discover our community's past natural heritage. Which plants were dominant then, and how does that compare to what is dominant today? How did our soils form, what did the land look like long ago, and why is the land shaped the way it is today?

*Note: The following outline aligns to Form H, "Standards-Based Unit Checklist," on page 40.

Having become familiar with both our past and present natural heritage, we will then explore our community's past and present cultural heritage and the interrelationships that exist between our local natural and cultural heritage. We will study the historical events that shaped our present-day community and the ways in which our natural heritage has influenced our community's development over time. We will also study how our ancestors lived and utilized the land, the foods they gathered, and the foods they were able to grow. We will compare and contrast our ancestors' way of life with the way we live today. What has and has not changed over time, and why? We will discover answers to the questions, "Who were we?" and "Who are we?"

The next stop on our journey will be to further explore our community's cultural past through working with our local elders and other community members. We will learn the traditional stories, skills, and knowledge of our ancestors and, in so doing, serve our community by helping to sustain its unique identity and local culture.

Throughout our experience we will be engaged in activities that cut across the disciplines, accommodate the multiple intelligences, and address and assess multiple standards. Projects and activities will include mapmaking, murals, diaries, storytelling, research, oral history, interviewing elders, cooperative learning, apprenticeships, peer teaching, problem solving, and service-learning.

The fall chapter of our story will end with our grand culminating activity, "Our Community's Story: A Community Heritage Festival." Students, parents, teachers, and community members will all share in demonstrating the knowledge they've acquired, the skills they've learned, and the standards they've attained during this eight-week segment of their recreation of their community's story.

Essential Questions

- What is the story of our community?
- How did our ancestors adapt to this northern temperate-forest environment, sustain themselves and others through the seasons, and sustain our community over time?

Focusing Questions

- How did our ancestors prepare for winter?
- In what ways did they aid and support one another?
- How does our way of life and relationship to the land compare to our ancestors' way of life and relationship to the land?

Standards

We will be addressing and ultimately assessing all fourteen embedded standards (see Embedded Standards list on page29) throughout our yearlong unit. Our special focus during our eight-week Fall Strand will be on the following standards:

1.18 Information Technology
2.2 Problem Solving
3.10 Teamwork
6.6 Being a Historian
7.1 Scientific Method

Goals

- Students will attain the above standards.
- Students will learn the local history and cultural heritage of their community through research and documenting the stories of elders and other community members.
- Students will be able to answer the essential and focusing questions.
- Students will develop a greater appreciation of their cultural heritage.
- Students will develop a greater understanding of the interrelationships between the land and their community.
- Students will develop a desire to serve and sustain their community.

Rationale

Cultural literacy units

- provide authentic, personally relevant learning opportunities for students and the community;
- address multiple standards;
- reconnect students to their natural and cultural heritage and the interrelationships that exist between the two;
- revitalize school-community partnerships;
- establish a sense of place, identity, purpose, and belonging for all students.

Culminating Activities

We will culminate each season with a celebration of understanding place that focuses on the natural and cultural heritage of our community and the stories, skills, and traditional knowledge of our ancestors. Students, parents, teachers, and community members will share what they've discovered and demonstrate the standards they've attained through multiple intelligence projects of their choice (exhibits, storytelling, drama, visual arts projects [photos, video, drawings, models], music). Our fall culminating activity will be titled "Our Community's Story: A Community Heritage Festival."

Assessment Plan

Our purposeful, systematic plan for assessing student progress on an ongoing basis will include using a variety and balance of assessment activities, tasks, and tools (rubrics and checklists [scoring guides]). Assessment will include a balance of both task-specific and generalized-standard assessment as well as periodic affective and student self-assessment.

Our unit will begin with

- assessment of students' existing knowledge (preassessment);
- assessment of what students hope to learn;

- introduction to the standards and criteria students will be working toward and the corresponding rubrics and checklists with which the students will be assessed and assess themselves;
- introduction to the culminating activity, its purpose, and the criteria students are expected to meet.

Unit Outline

Note: Eleven assessment activities have been formatted as detailed lesson plans and are found on pages 145 to 165. All assessment tasks and tools mentioned are found in Appendix B.

Week 1

Our Community's Story

1. Introduce students to the story they are about to re-create over the next eight weeks.
2. Ask students to create their individual community story portfolios in which they will keep an ongoing collection of artifacts of their projects and performances as well as additional assessments of their overall progress.
3. Preassess students using a "Community Now and Before" task to determine existing knowledge and pre- and misconceptions.
4. Preassess students using a KWL to determine what students want to know or know more about local history and cultural heritage.
5. Introduce (or reintroduce) standards 1.18, 2.2, 3.10, 6.6, and 7.1, their criteria, and their respective rubrics and checklists.
6. Introduce the culminating activity, its purpose, and its criteria checklist.
7. Identify and begin preparing your community coordinator (see Step 2, page 47).
8. Reserve a future date for the unit's culminating community heritage festival.

Week 2

Our Community's Natural Heritage

1. Brainstorm with students a list of words and ideas they believe capture the essence of their community. Allow students to explain their choice of words. Anecdotally note affective responses that reveal students' feelings. In cooperative groups ask students to discern those words and ideas that represent natural heritage (flora, fauna, terrain, water, soil, climate, weather) from those representing cultural (human) heritage (see "Heritage Brainstorm Sort" in Appendix B, [age 184). Discuss which of the two was more represented and possible reasons why. Anecdotally assess for existing knowledge and assess Teamwork using 3.10 rubrics.
2. Assessment activity: "Mapping our Community's Past Natural Heritage" (page 148). (*Note:* An assessment activity is an enabling activity that involves student-teacher interaction and is deliberately designed to result in products or performances that can be used to assess student progress.) In cooperative groups ask students to use ideas from their brainstorming session to direct them as they research their community's present natural assets. Then challenge students to create a map representing the present-day natural heritage of their community. Use an appropriate task (e.g., journal entry, concept web) and their maps to assess students' application of knowledge learned in previous lesson and assess Problem Solving and Information Technology using 2.2 checklist and 1.18 checklist.
3. Invite a local expert to speak on the natural history of their community.
4. Assessment activity: "Researching Our Community's Past Natural Heritage" (see page 146). Ask students to research the past local natural heritage of various time periods and compare and contrast with present-day natural heritage.

Anecdotally note application of knowledge learned in previous lessons and assess Being a Historian using 6.6 rubric and checklist.

5. Assessment activity: "Mapping Our Community's Past Natural Heritage" (see page 148). With students in cooperative groups, ask them to create maps representing the past natural heritage of their place over time, compare and contrast them with their present-day natural heritage maps, and predict what a map of the future might look like. Use maps and an accompanying task to assess students' application of knowledge learned in previous lessons and assess Problem Solving using 2.2 checklist and Teamwork using 3.10 rubrics.

6. Revisit KWL and culminating activity checklist.

Week 3

Our Community's Cultural Heritage

1. Revisit last week's brainstorming session and review words and ideas that reflect the present-day cultural heritage of the students' community. Anecdotally assess understanding of the term *culture* and the difference between cultural and natural heritage.

2. Assessment activity: "Local Cultural Heritage Mural" (see page 150). In cooperative groups ask students to use ideas from their brainstorming session to direct them as they search for information on their community's present cultural assets. Then challenge students to create a mural that reflects their community's present-day culture. Use murals to assess students' acquisition of knowledge and assess Teamwork using 3.10 rubrics.

3. Invite a local expert to serve as a guest speaker on the cultural heritage of their community.

4. Assessment activity: "Researching Our Community's Cultural Past" (see page 152). Ask students to research past local cultural heritage and compare and contrast with present-day culture. Use an appropriate task to assess application of

knowledge learned in previous lessons and assess Information Technology using 1.18 checklist.

5. Assessment activity: "Mural Timelines of our Community's Cultural Past" (see page 154). In cooperative groups ask students to create a mural(s) that reflects their community's cultural past over time on a wall adjacent to their present-day cultural mural, compare and contrast the two murals, and predict what a mural of the future would portray. Anecdotally assess application of knowledge learned in previous lessons and assess Problem Solving using 2.2 checklist.
6. Revisit "Community Now and Before" task.

Week 4

Preparing for Winter

1. Preassessment task. Ask students to use their past natural heritage maps and cultural heritage murals and begin creating an alternating voice diary in which they simultaneously describe how both they (their family) and their community "ancestors" prepare(d) for winter. Use diaries to assess existing knowledge, affect, and application of knowledge learned in previous lessons.
2. Introduce students to the interviewing process (see Step 3, page 65).
3. Assessment activity: "Elder Interviews" (page 158). Ask students to interview a community elder (neighbor, grandparent, historical society referral) and document stories on how they and their family and friends prepared for winter when they were children. Have students share these stories with the class and compare and contrast with what they wrote in their diaries. Anecdotally assess application of knowledge learned in previous lessons and assess Teamwork and Being a Historian using 3.10 rubrics and 6.6 rubric and checklist.

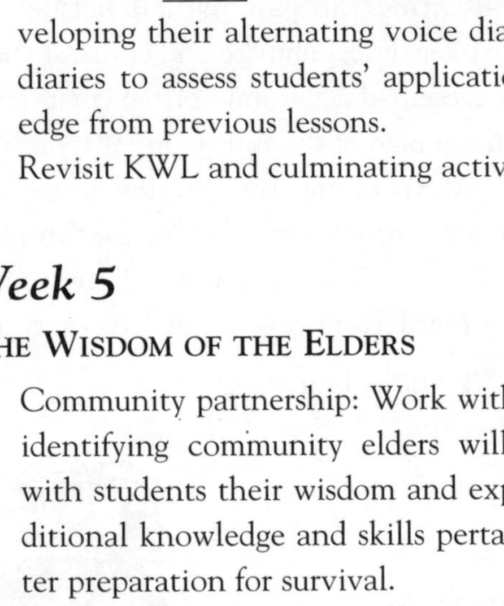

4. Assessment activity: "Preparing for Winter: The Diaries of ______." Ask students to continue developing their alternating voice diaries. Use the diaries to assess students' application of knowledge from previous lessons.
5. Revisit KWL and culminating activity checklist.

Week 5

The Wisdom of the Elders

1. Community partnership: Work with students on identifying community elders willing to share with students their wisdom and expertise in traditional knowledge and skills pertaining to winter preparation for survival.
2. Meet with interested elders and help them prepare for their role in this community project (see Step 4, page 75).
3. Assessment activity: "Community Map and Mural Exhibition." Invite those elders (and others) to a map and mural showing in which students (cooperative groups) present their projects and elders collaborate with the groups on brainstorming ways to further develop the community maps and murals. Use students' presentations to assess their application of knowledge from previous lessons and assess Being a Historian, Problem Solving, and Teamwork using 6.6 rubric and checklist, 2.2 checklist, and 3.10 rubrics.
4. Assessment activity: "Researching Traditional Skills of Our Ancestors" (see page 158). In cooperative groups ask students to conduct initial research and write a report on a traditional skill of their choice which they want to experience through apprenticeship with one of the participating elders. Anecdotally assess affect and assess Information Technology using 1.18 checklist.
5. Revisit culminating activity checklist.

Week 6

Traditional Skills and Knowledge

1. Assessment activity: "Apprenticeships" (see page 160). Ask students as they participate in a one-week apprenticeship to maintain a daily log documenting what they learn, discoveries they make, questions they have, and approaches they might take to pass this tradition on to future generations, and why. Use students' logs and elder conferences to assess student affect, acquisition of knowledge, and project success, and assess Scientific Method using 7.1 rubrics and video documentation.
2. Assessment activity: "Master Teachers" (see page 162). In cooperative groups ask students to plan, organize, and conduct a peer apprenticeship for the craft they've learned. Anecdotally assess affect; use elder conferences and videotaped presentations to assess knowledge acquisition, and assess Teamwork and Problem Solving using 3.10 rubrics and 2.2 checklist.

Week 7

Traditional Skills and Knowledge

1. Repeat Week 6 with a second apprenticeship.
2. Revisit culminating activity checklist.

Week 8

Culminating Activity

1. Assessment activity: "Our Community's Story: A Community Heritage Festival" (see page 164). In cooperative groups ask students to develop a culminating project for the fall strand of their "Our Community's Story" unit. Remind students to continue to refer to their culminating activity checklist as they design their final demonstrations of sense of place. Videotape the festival for assessment and documentary purposes.
2. Postassessment: Conduct a final assessment of student progress using the Fall Strand culminating activity checklist (page 166); 1.18, 2.2, 3.10, 6.6, 7.1 rubrics and checklists; "Community Now and Before" task; and unit KWL.
3. Unit assessment: Using the "Unit Assessment Form" (see page 179) postassess the Fall Strand portion of the unit before planning and beginning the Winter and Spring Strands.

WEEK 2
Mapping Our Community's Natural Heritage

Standard(s) Being Addressed

Fall Focus Standards

- 1.18 Information Technology
- 2.2 Problem Solving
- 3.10 Teamwork
- 6.6 Being a Historian

Additional Embedded Standards

- 1.19 Research
- 4.1 Service
- 4.5 Continuity and Change
- 7.13 Organisms, Evolution, and Interdependence
- 4.6 Understanding Place
- 6.8 Movements and Settlements
- 7.11 Systems: Analysis

Inquiry/Focusing Questions

What makes up the landscape that surrounds our community?

What are our community's natural assets?

How is our surrounding landscape impacting our community?

How is our community impacting our surrounding landscape?

Why is there such a strong connection between the natural heritage and cultural heritage of a community?

Topic

Our community's present surrounding landscape, its natural assets, and the interrelationships that exist between our community and its surrounding landscape.

Materials

reference materials documenting local natural history (state agency documents, local planning commission maps, GIS maps, town maps, aerial photographs, local environmental organization surveys)

plant and animal field guides

logs (composition booklets)

graph paper

variety of art media and construction materials

Procedures

1. Divide students into heterogeneous groups (encourage cooperative learning skills and division of labor).
2. Review with students the definition of natural heritage and the various elements of natural heritage (flora, fauna, terrain, water, soil, weather, climate).
3. Begin collecting data, starting with a survey of the school grounds and its surrounding landscape. Ask students to record general observations of local species in their logs and map the school landscape on their graph paper. Remind students that they will ultimately be using the data they collect and the maps they draw to create three-dimensional panorama maps of their community's natural heritage.
4. Extend data collection to include the broader town/community by taking a field trip around town, recording local species and mapping the broader landscape.
5. Further identify the community's surrounding landscape and natural heritage by having students supplement their data collection using the references listed under Materials.
6. Ask students to synthesize the data collected in their logs, their graph-paper maps, and their reference research and use that combined information to create three-dimensional maps that represent their community's surrounding landscape, natural assets, and local species. (*Note:* Each cooperative group could create its own map or each could create one part of a whole-class map.)
7. Engage students in a discussion on the activity's focusing questions.
8. Assess students' acquisition of knowledge and progress toward attaining the standards.

Task-Specific Assessment

(products, performances, tasks, scoring guides [rubrics/checklists], anecdotal observations)

logs
graph-paper maps
three-dimensional maps
anecdotal observations
concept webs

Generalized-Standard Assessment

2.2 Problem-solving checklist

1.18 Information Technology checklist

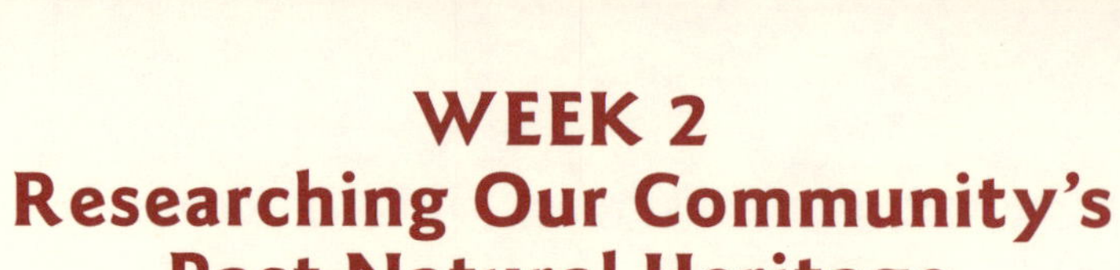

WEEK 2
Researching Our Community's Past Natural Heritage

Standard(s) Being Addressed

Fall Focus Standards

1.18	Information Technology	2.2	Problem Solving
6.6	Being a Historian		

Additional Embedded Standards

1.19	Research	6.8	Movements and Settlements
4.5	Continuity and Change	7.11	Systems: Analysis
4.6	Understanding Place		
7.13	Organisms, Evolution, and Interdependence		

Inquiry/Focusing Questions

What was the landscape like that surrounded our ancestral community?

What were our ancestral community's natural assets?

How did the surrounding landscape impact our ancestral community?

How did our ancestral community impact its surrounding landscape?

Why is there such a strong connection between the natural heritage and cultural heritage of a community?

Topic

Our community's past surrounding landscape, its former natural assets, and the interrelationships that existed between our past community and its surrounding landscape

Materials

reference materials documenting past local natural history (state agency documents, local planning commission maps, historical society archives, geological surveys, children's local historical fiction)

tape players (for students choosing to interview as a way of gathering qualitative data) media to accommodate multiple intelligence demonstrations (e.g., art supplies, construction materials, musical instruments, writing tools)

Procedures

1. Provide students with the references listed under Materials and ask students to research the past natural heritage of their local community. One possible timeline of historical periods for students to represent might be: Paleo-Indian, Archaic Indian, Woodland Indian, Fur Trade, Colonial, Preindustrial Agriculture/Forestry, Industrial Revolution. Remind students that ultimately they will share what they learn with their classmates. (*Note:* Each student could be assigned all the major time periods being represented in this project, or the various time periods could be divided among the students.)
2. On completing their research, ask students to plan and organize a multiple intelligence demonstration of their choice in which they compare and contrast their community's present natural heritage with that of the time period(s) they researched.
3. Ask students to present their projects to their classmates.
4. Engage students in a culminating discussion on the activity's focusing questions and the continuity and change of their community's natural heritage and landscape over time.
5. Assess students' acquisition of knowledge and progress toward attaining the standards.

Task-Specific Assessment

(products, performances, tasks, scoring guides [rubrics/checklists], anecdotal observations)

multiple intelligence demonstrations

whole-class discussion

anecdotal observations

Generalized-Standard Assessment

6.6 Being a Historian rubric/checklist

WEEK 2
Mapping Our Community's Past Natural Heritage

Standard(s) Being Addressed

Fall Focus Standards

1.18	Information Technology	3.10	Teamwork
2.2	Problem Solving	6.6	Being a Historian

Additional Embedded Standards

1.19	Research	4.6	Understanding Place
4.1	Service	6.8	Movements and Settlements
4.5	Continuity and Change	7.11	Systems: Analysis
7.13	Organisms, Evolution, and Interdependence		

Inquiry/Focusing Questions

What was the landscape like that surrounded our ancestral community?

What were our ancestral community's natural assets?

How did the surrounding landscape impact our ancestral community?

How did our ancestral community impact its surrounding landscape?

Why is there such a strong connection between the natural heritage and cultural heritage of a community?

Topic

Our ancestral community's surrounding landscape, its natural assets, and the interrelationships that existed between our ancestral community and its surrounding landscape

Materials

variety of art media and construction materials

information gathered during previous lesson

present-day natural heritage maps completed earlier

Procedures

1. Divide students into heterogeneous groups (encourage cooperative learning skills and division of labor).
2. Ask students to synthesize the data collected from their previous research of past natural heritage, their classmate's presentations, and class discussion and use that combined information to create three-dimensional maps that represent their ancestral community's surrounding landscape, natural assets, and local species. (*Note:* Each co-operative group could create its own map of a specific time period, or each group could create one part [time period] of a whole-class map. In either case, a timeline of past natural heritage maps will result.)
3. Once maps are completed, revisit your earlier discussion on the activity's focusing questions and comparing and contrasting your community's past and present natural heritage and ask groups to predict what a map of the future would portray.
4. Discuss with the class the various predictions.
5. Assess students' acquisition of knowledge and progress toward attaining the standards.

Task-Specific Assessment

(products, performances, tasks, scoring guides [rubrics/checklists], anecdotal observations)

three-dimensional maps

Venn diagram (past/present comparison)

predictions

anecdotal observations of class discussion

Generalized-Standard Assessment

2.2	Problem-solving checklist	3.10	Teamwork rubrics

WEEK 3
Local Cultural Heritage Mural

Standard(s) Being Addressed

Fall Focus Standards

1.18 Information Technology
2.2 Problem Solving
3.10 Teamwork
6.6 Being a Historian

Additional Embedded Standards

1.19 Research
4.1 Service
4.5 Continuity and Change
4.6 Understanding Place
6.8 Movements and Settlements
7.11 Systems: Analysis

Inquiry/Focusing Questions

What makes up the cultural landscape of our community?

What are our community's cultural assets?

How is the culture of our community impacting our community's surrounding landscape?

How is our community's surrounding landscape impacting the culture of our community?

Why is there such a strong connection between the cultural heritage and natural heritage of a community?

Topic

Our community's present cultural landscape, its cultural assets, and the interrelationships that exist between our community's cultural heritage and its surrounding landscape

Materials

reference materials documenting local culture (children's local contemporary fiction, chamber of commerce information, town reports, local demographic surveys, local newspapers, business directories)

variety of art media and construction materials

logs (composition booklets)

Procedures

1. Divide students into heterogeneous groups (encourage cooperative learning skills and division of labor).
2. Review with students the definition of culture and the various categories of human culture (e.g., lifestyle, government, economy, religion, arts, architecture).
3. Begin collecting data, starting with a survey of the school and school neighborhood. Ask students to record general observations of local culture in their logs. Remind students that they will ultimately be using the data they collect to create a mural of their community's cultural heritage.
4. Extend data collection to include the broader town/community by taking a field trip around town, recording additional examples of local culture.
5. Further identify the community's cultural landscape by having students supplement their data collection using the references listed under Materials
6. Ask students to synthesize the data collected in their logs and their reference research and use that combined information to create a mural that represents their community's present cultural landscape. (*Note:* Each cooperative group could create its own mural, or each group could create one part of a whole-class mural.)
7. Engage students in a discussion on the activity's focusing questions.
8. Assess students' acquisition of knowledge and progress toward attaining the standards.

Task-Specific Assessment

(products, performances, tasks, scoring guides [rubrics/checklists], anecdotal observations)

logs

murals

anecdotal observations of group work

whole-class discussions

Generalized-Standard Assessment

3.10 Teamwork rubrics

WEEK 3
Researching Our Community's Cultural Past

Standard(s) Being Addressed

Fall Focus Standards

1.18 Information Technology
6.6 Being a Historian
2.2 Problem Solving

Additional Embedded Standards

1.19 Research
4.5 Continuity and Change
4.6 Understanding Place
6.8 Movements and Settlements
7.11 Systems: Analysis

Inquiry/Focusing Questions

What was the cultural landscape of our ancestral community?

What were our ancestral community's cultural assets?

How did the culture of our ancestral community impact its surrounding landscape?

How did the surrounding environment impact our cultural past?

Why is there such a strong connection between the cultural heritage and natural heritage of a community?

Topic

Our community's past cultural landscape, its former cultural assets, and the interrelationships that existed between our past community and its surrounding landscape.

Materials

reference materials documenting past local cultural heritage (historical society archives, children's local historical fiction, film documentaries, grandparents' or community elders' memorabilia)

tape players (for students choosing to interview as a way of gathering qualitative data)

media to accommodate multiple intelligence demonstrations (art supplies, construction materials, musical instruments, writing utensils)

Procedures

1. Provide students with the references listed under Materials and ask students to research the past cultural heritage of their local community. One possible timeline of historical periods for students to represent might be: Paleo-Indian, Archaic Indian, Woodland Indian, Fur Trade, Colonial, Preindustrial Agriculture/forestry, Industrial Revolution. Remind students that ultimately they will share what they learn with their classmates. (*Note:* Each student could be assigned all the major time periods represented in this project, or the various time periods could be divided among the students.)
2. On completing their research, ask students to plan and organize a multiple intelligence demonstration of their choice in which they compare and contrast their community's present cultural heritage with that of the time period(s) they researched.
3. Ask students to present their projects to their classmates.
4. Engage students in a culminating discussion on the activity's focusing questions and the continuity and change of their community's cultural heritage over time.
5. Assess students' acquisition of knowledge and progress toward attaining the standards.

Task-Specific Assessment

(products, performances, tasks, scoring guides [rubrics/checklists], anecdotal observations)

multiple intelligence demonstrations

whole-class discussion

Venn diagram (past/present comparison)

anecdotal observations

Generalized-Standard Assessment

1.18 Information Technology checklist

WEEK 3
Mural Timelines of Our Community's Cultural Past

Standard(s) Being Addressed

Fall Focus Standards

1.18	Information Technology	3.10	Teamwork
2.2	Problem Solving	6.6	Being a Historian

Additional Embedded Standards

1.19	Research	4.6	Understanding Place
4.1	Service	6.8	Movements and Settlements
4.5	Continuity and Change	7.11	Systems: Analysis

Inquiry/Focusing Questions

What was the cultural landscape of our ancestral community?

What were our ancestral community's cultural assets?

How did the culture of our ancestral community impact its surrounding landscape?

How did the surrounding landscape impact the culture heritage of our ancestral community?

Why is there such a strong connection between the cultural heritage and natural heritage of a community?

Topic

Our cultural heritage, our ancestral community's cultural assets, and the interrelationships that existed between our ancestral community and its surrounding landscape

Materials

variety of art media and construction materials

information gathered during previous lesson

present-day cultural heritage murals completed earlier

Procedures

1. Divide students into heterogeneous groups (encourage cooperative learning skills and division of labor).
2. Ask students to synthesize the data collected from their previous research of past cultural heritage, their classmates' presentations, and class discussion and use that combined information to create a mural(s) that represents their ancestral community's cultural heritage. (*Note:* Each cooperative group could create its own mural of a specific time period, or a each group could create one part [time period] of a whole-class mural. In either case, a timeline of past cultural heritage murals will result.)
3. Once murals are completed, revisit your earlier discussion on the activity's focusing questions and comparing and contrasting your community's past and present cultural heritage, then ask groups to predict what a mural of the future might contain.
4. Discuss the various predictions.
5. Assess students' acquisition of knowledge and progress toward attaining the standards.

Task-Specific Assessment

(products, performances, tasks, scoring guides [rubrics/checklists], anecdotal observations)

murals

predictions

anecdotal observations of class discussion

Generalized-Standard Assessment

2.2 Problem-solving checklist

WEEK 4
Elder Interviews

Standard(s) Being Addressed

Fall Focus Standards

1.18 Information Technology
3.10 Teamwork
2.2 Problem Solving
6.6 Being a Historian

Additional Embedded Standards

1.19 Research
4.1 Service
4.5 Continuity and Change
4.6 Understanding Place
6.8 Movements and Settlements
7.11 Systems: Analysis

Inquiry/Focusing Questions

How did our ancestors learn to live in this place?

What was our ancestral culture like?

How did our ancestors use and sustain the land?

How did the land shape the way our ancestors lived?

What lessons might we learn from the wisdom and experience of our elders?

Topic

A look through the eyes of our elders at our community's cultural heritage and the ways in which our ancestors were connected to the land

Materials

tape recorders

logs (composition booklets)

alternating voice diaries (see Fall Strand, Week Four, number 1)

Procedures

1. Divide students into heterogeneous groups (encourage cooperative learning skills and division of labor). (*Note:* Logistics will influence whether students engage in this activity individually or in cooperative groups.)
2. Review with students the interviewing skills they learned during their introduction to the interviewing process (see Fall Strand: Week Four, number 2).
3. Ask students/groups to arrange an interview with a grandparent, elderly neighbor, or friend, generate a list of interview questions particular to the topic they are researching, then have students share their questions and solicit feedback from their classmates on possible revisions.
4. Conduct elder interviews.
5. Ask students to compare and contrast what they learned from their interviews with what they have written so far in their alternating voice diaries.
6. Ask students/groups to present to their classmates the results of their interviews and what they discovered when they compared them with the alternating voice diaries they began earlier.
7. Discuss with the class the patterns and general findings that emerged from the interviews.
8. Engage students in a discussion of the activity's focusing questions.
9. Assess students' acquisition of knowledge and progress toward attaining the standards.

Task-Specific Assessment

(products, performances, tasks, scoring guides [rubrics/checklists], anecdotal observations)

interview questions

interview logs

alternating voice diaries

anecdotal observations of group presentations and discussions

Generalized-Standard Assessment

3.10 Teamwork rubrics

6.6 Being a Historian rubric/checklist

WEEK 5
Researching Traditional Skills of Our Ancestors

Standard(s) Being Addressed

Fall Focus Standards

1.18 Information Technology
6.6 Being a Historian
2.2 Problem Solving

Additional Embedded Standards

1.19 Research
4.5 Continuity and Change
4.6 Understanding Place
6.8 Movements and Settlements
7.11 Systems: Analysis

Inquiry/Focusing Questions

What skills did our ancestors need to survive in this place?

In what ways were those skills connected with the land?

How did those skills sustain our ancestors and their community?

Are any of those skills still in use today? Why or why not?

For those skills not still in use, are any worth bringing back/holding onto? Why or why not?

How does our relationship to the land compare with the relationship our ancestors had with the land?

Topic

The traditional knowledge and skills of our community's cultural past and the interdependence between our ancestors and the land on which they lived

Materials

reference materials documenting past local cultural heritage (historical society archives, children's local historical fiction, film documentaries, grandparents' or elders' memorabilia, museum artifact kits)

tape players (for students choosing to interview as a way of gathering qualitative data)

information from interviews conducted earlier (see Fall Strand: Week Four, number 4)

Procedures

1. Provide students with the references listed under Materials and ask students to research the traditional skill(s) from their community's past, which they have selected for their upcoming apprenticeship (see Fall Strand: Week Five, number 1 and Week Six, number 1). One possible timeline of historical periods for student apprenticeships to span might be: Paleo-Indian, Archaic Indian, Woodland Indian, Fur Trade, Colonial, Preindustrial Agriculture/Forestry, Industrial Revolution.
2. On completing their research, ask students to organize the information they have gathered in the form of a report to be presented to their classmates as part of their Master Teacher project (see Fall Strand: Week Six, number 2).
3. Engage students in a discussion on the activity's focusing questions.
4. Assess students' affect, acquisition of knowledge, and progress toward attaining the standards.

Task-Specific Assessment

(products, performances, tasks, scoring guides [rubrics/checklists], anecdotal observations)

research report

affective survey

anecdotal observations

Generalized-Standard Assessment

1.18 Information Technology checklist

WEEKS 6 and 7
Apprenticeships

Standard(s) Being Addressed

Fall Focus Standards

2.2 Problem Solving
3.10 Teamwork
6.6 Being a Historian
7.1 Scientific Method

Additional Embedded Standards

4.1 Service
4.5 Continuity and Change
4.6 Understanding Place
6.8 Movements and Settlements
7.11 Systems: Analysis

Inquiry/Focusing Questions

What skills did our ancestors need to survive in this place?

In what ways were those skills connected with the land?

How did those skills sustain our ancestors and their community?

Are any of those skills still in use today? Why or why not?

For those skills not still in use, are any worth bringing back or holding onto? Why or why not?

If I had been alive back then, which skill(s) might I have been a master in, and why?

How does our relationship to the land compare with the relationship our ancestors had with the land?

Topic

Students participating in apprenticeships relating to the traditional knowledge and skills of our community's cultural past and exploring the interdependence that existed between our ancestors and the land on which they lived

Materials

logs (composition booklets)

materials for participating elders' respective apprenticeships (assist elders in gathering necessary materials)

video recorder

Procedures

1. Schedule sufficient time and organize sufficient space within which the apprenticeships can successfully take place.
2. Determine student-elder partnerships based on the students' requests for apprenticeships.
3. Meet with participating elders one more time as a follow-up to your Elder Preparation meeting earlier (see Fall Strand: Week 5, number 2). Discuss any remaining questions or concerns, logistics (e.g., rooms in which they will be located, number of students they will be working with), and any final preparation help needed.
4. Provide students with apprenticeship logs (composition booklets) and ask them to maintain a daily log documenting what they learn during their apprenticeship, discoveries they make, questions they have, and approaches they might take to pass this tradition on to future generations, and why.
5. Conduct apprenticeships.
6. Periodically conference with participating elders to assess project success.
7. Engage students and elders in a discussion on the activity's focusing questions.
8. Assess students' affect, acquisition of knowledge, and progress toward attaining the standards.

Task-Specific Assessment

(products, performances, tasks, scoring guides [rubrics/checklists], anecdotal observations)

apprenticeship logs

affective survey

video recording

anecdotal observations

conferences with elders

Generalized-Standard Assessment

7.1 Scientific Method rubrics

WEEKS 6 and 7
Master Teachers

Standard(s) Being Addressed

Fall Focus Standards

2.2 Problem Solving
3.10 Teamwork
6.6 Being a Historian
7.1 Scientific Method

Additional Embedded Standards

4.1 Service
4.5 Continuity and Change
4.6 Understanding Place
6.8 Movements and Settlements
7.11 Systems: Analysis

Inquiry/Focusing Questions

What skills did our ancestors need to survive in this place?

In what ways were those skills connected with the land?

How did those skills sustain our ancestors and their community?

Are any of those skills still in use today? Why or why not?

For those skills not still in use, are any worth bringing back or holding onto? Why or why not?

How does our relationship to the land compare to the relationship our ancestors had with the land?

Topic

Students conducting workshops for their peers on the traditional knowledge and skills of our community's cultural past and the interdependence between our ancestors and the land on which they lived

Materials

variety of media to accommodate multiple approaches students might take in presenting their Master Teacher workshop for peers (chart paper and easel, overhead projector and transparencies, markers, slide projector for students choosing to use accompanying slides, various software programs such as Hyperstudio and Power Point)

video recorder

Procedures

1. Schedule sufficient time and organize sufficient space within which the Master Teacher workshops can successfully take place.
2. Devise a rotating schedule which maximizes opportunities for students to experience as many different peer workshops as possible.
3. Invite participating elders to attend student workshops.
4. Provide students with presentation materials of their choice and time to plan and organize their presentations. Also, with the help of your participating elders, assist students in obtaining enough supplies for their peers to each be able to make or do the skill being taught.
5. Conduct Master Teacher peer workshops. Ask students to demonstrate their craft and share the research reports they did earlier (see Fall Strand: Week 5, number 4) on the history of their traditional skill.
6. Conference with elders to assess student performance and acquisition of knowledge.
7. Engage students and elders in a discussion on the activity's focusing questions.
8. Assess students' affect, acquisition of knowledge, and progress toward attaining the standards.

Task-Specific Assessment

(products, performances, tasks, scoring guides [rubrics/checklists], anecdotal observations)

Master Teacher workshops

elder conferences

video recordings

anecdotal observations

Generalized-Standard Assessment

2.2	Problem-solving checklist	3.10	Teamwork rubrics

WEEK 8
Our Community's Story: A Community Heritage Festival

Standard(s) Being Addressed

Fall Focus Standards

1.18 Information Technology
2.2 Problem Solving
7.1 Scientific Method
3.10 Teamwork
6.6 Being a Historian

Additional Embedded Standards

1.19 Research
4.1 Service
4.5 Continuity and Change
4.6 Understanding Place
7.13 Organisms, Evolution, and Interdependence
6.8 Movements and Settlements
7.2 Investigation
7.9 Probability and Statistics
7.11 Systems: Analysis

Inquiry/Focusing Questions

What is the story of our community?

How did our ancestors adapt to this northern temperate forest environment, sustain themselves and others through the seasons (i.e., winter), and sustain our community over time?

Why is there such a strong connection between the cultural heritage and natural heritage of a community?

How does our relationship to the land compare to the relationship our ancestors had

Topic

Culminating festival with student exhibits that reflect our community's story and demonstrate students' acquisition of knowledge and progress toward the standards

Materials

variety of supplies and media for exhibits and advertisements

multiple copies of culminating activity checklists for community participants to use in assessing students' exhibits

students' community story portfolios for them to use in developing their exhibits

video recorder

Procedures

1. Ask students in advance to create and distribute fliers and posters advertising their upcoming community heritage festival.
2. Schedule sufficient time and organize sufficient space within which students can successfully develop their culminating exhibits.
3. Invite participating elders to assist students in developing their exhibits.
4. Arrange ahead of time for refreshments to be provided during the festival.
5. Designate student greeters to welcome community members and hand out culminating activity checklists to those attendees who would like to volunteer to help assess the students' exhibits.
6. Designate students to videotape the festival.
7. Designate student teams to help with various aspects of cleanup once the festival is over.
8. Schedule adequate time for students/elders to set up their exhibits before the start of the festival.
9. Once exhibits are set up, ask students to conduct a self-assessment using the culminating activity checklist.
10. Celebrate your community's heritage. Let the festival begin!
11. During (if logistics allow) or following the festival, engage students and elders in a discussion on the culminating activity's focusing questions.
12. After the festival is over and clean up is complete, allow students to view the video and see the results of the community assessments of their exhibits.
13. Conduct a final assessment of students' affect, acquisition of knowledge, and progress toward attaining the standards.

Task-Specific Assessment

(products, performances, tasks, scoring guides [rubrics/checklists], anecdotal observations)

culminating exhibits video recordings anecdotal observations

self-assessment checklists community assessment checklists

"Community Now and Before" tasks unit KWLs affective surveys

Generalized-Standard Assessment

1.18	Information Technology checklists	3.10	Teamwork rubrics
2.2	Problem-solving checklists	6.6	Being a Historian rubrics
7.1	Scientific Method rubrics		

OUR COMMUNITY'S STORY: PREPARING FOR WINTER
Fall Strand Culminating Activity Checklist

Name ______________________________ Date __________

Activity ______________________________

_____ Demonstrates knowledge of our community's past and present culture

_____ Demonstrates knowledge of our community's past and present natural heritage

_____ Answers the unit's essential and focusing questions

_____ Demonstrates evidence of using information technology (1.18)

_____ Demonstrates evidence of problem solving (2.2)

_____ Demonstrates evidence of teamwork (3.10)

_____ Demonstrates evidence of being a historian (6.6)

_____ Demonstrates evidence of using scientific methods (7.1)

_____ Purpose is obvious

_____ Information is clear

_____ Presentation is effective and audience-considerate

_____ Effort demonstrates interest, enthusiasm, and investment

_____ Reflects student expertise

Winter Strand

A Sample Eight-Week Unit Outline

Story

Our story (unit*) will be a yearlong re-creation of how our ancestors learned to live on this land and make this place their home. It will be based on the rich history and cultural heritage of our local community and begin with an exploration of our homeland's natural assets. We will get to know our land's flora, fauna, terrain, and climate. We will also become familiar with our community's place within our larger watershed. In short, we will explore the question, "Where are we?"

Once we know the natural habitats within and around our community, we will then take a trip back in time and discover our community's past natural heritage. Which plants were dominant then, and how does that compare to what is dominant today? How did our soils form, what did the land look like long ago, and why is the land shaped the way it is, today?

Having become familiar with both our past and present natural heritage, we will then explore our community's past and present cultural heritage and the interrelationships that exist between our local natural and cultural heritage. We will study the historical events that shaped our present-day community and the ways in which our natural heritage has influenced our community's development over time. We will also study how our ancestors lived and utilized the land: the foods they gathered and the foods they were able to grow. We will compare and contrast our ancestors' way of life with the way we live today. What has and has not changed over time, and why? We will discover answers to the questions, "Who were we?" and "Who are we?"

The next stop on our journey will be to further explore our community's cultural past through working with our local elders and other community members. We will learn the traditional stories, skills, and knowledge of our ancestors, and in so doing, serve our community by helping to sustain its unique identity and local culture.

**Note:* The following outline aligns to Form H, "Standards-Based Unit Checklist," on page 40.

Throughout our experience, we will be engaged in activities that cut across the disciplines, accommodate the multiple intelligences, and address and assess multiple standards. Projects and activities will include mapmaking, murals, diaries, storytelling, research, oral history, interviewing elders, cooperative learning, apprenticeships, peer teaching, problem solving, and service-learning.

The winter chapter of our story will end with our grand culminating activity, "Cabin Wellness: A Community Celebration of Winter." Students, parents, teachers, and community members will all share in demonstrating the knowledge they've acquired, the skills they've learned, and the standards they've attained during this eight-week segment of their re-creation of their community's story.

Essential Questions

- What is the story of our community?
- How did our ancestors adapt to this northern temperate forest environment, sustain themselves and others through the seasons, and sustain our community over time?

Focusing Questions

- How did our ancestors live during winter?
- In what ways did they depend on one another?
- How does our way of life and relationship to the land in winter compare to our ancestors' way of life and relationship to the land during winter?

Standards

We will be addressing and ultimately assessing all fourteen embedded standards (see "Embedded Standards" list, page 29) throughout our yearlong unit. Our special focus during our eight-week Winter Strand will be on the following standards:

1.19 Research

3.9 Sustainability

3.10 Teamwork

4.5 Continuity and Change

6.8 Movements and Settlements

7.2 Investigation

Goals

- Students will attain the above standards.
- Students will learn the local history and cultural heritage of their community through research and documenting the stories of elders and other community members.
- Students will be able to answer the essential and focusing questions.
- Students will develop a greater appreciation of their cultural heritage.
- Students will develop a greater understanding of the interrelationships between the land and their community.
- Students will develop a desire to serve and sustain their community.

Rationale

Cultural literacy units

- provide authentic, personally relevant learning opportunities for students and the community;
- address multiple standards;
- reconnect students to their natural and cultural heritage and the interrelationships that exist between the two;
- revitalize school and community partnerships;
- establish a sense of place, identity, purpose, and belonging for all students.

Culminating Activities

We will culminate each season with a celebration of understanding place that focuses on the natural and cultural heritage of our community and the stories, skills, and traditional knowledge of our ancestors. Students, parents, teachers, and community members will share what they've discovered and demonstrate the standards they've attained through multiple intelligence projects of their choice (exhibits, storytelling, drama, visual arts projects [photos, video, drawings, models], music). Our winter culminating activity will be titled "Cabin Wellness: A Community Celebration of Winter."

Assessment Plan

Our purposeful, systematic plan for assessing student progress on an ongoing basis will include using a variety and balance of assessment activities, tasks, and tools (rubrics and checklists [scoring guides]). Assessment will include a balance of both task-specific and generalized-standard assessment as well as periodic affective and student self-assessment.

Our unit will begin with

- assessment of students' existing knowledge (preassessment);
- assessment of what students hope to learn;
- introduction to the standards and criteria students will be working toward and the corresponding rubrics and checklists with which the students will be assessed and assess themselves;
- introduction to the culminating activity, its purpose, and the criteria students are expected to meet.

Unit Outline

Note: All assessment tasks and tools mentioned are in Appendix B.

Week 1

Our Community's Story

1. Review with students the community story they re-created during the Fall Strand, then introduce the segment they will be recreating over the next eight weeks.
2. Preassess students using a Winter Calendar task (a log of projected daily/weekly winter activities and events) to determine existing knowledge and pre- and misconceptions about life in winter during the old days.
3. Preassess students using a KWL to determine what students want to know or know more about regarding local history and cultural heritage.
4. Introduce (or reintroduce) standards 1.19, 3.9, 3.10, 4.5, 6.8, and 7.2, their criteria and their respective rubrics and checklists.
5. Introduce the Winter Strand's culminating activity, its purpose, and its criteria checklist.
6. Reserve a future date for the Winter Strand's culminating activity: "Cabin Wellness: A Community Celebration of Winter."

Week 2

Our Community's Natural History in Winter

1. Review with students the list of words and ideas from their original Fall Strand brainstorming session that captured the essence of their community's natural heritage (flora, fauna, terrain, water, soil, climate, weather). In cooperative groups ask students to come to a consensus on what land-related activity they think most impacts the life of their community during the winter months. Anecdotally assess for existing knowledge and assess Teamwork using 3.10 rubrics.
2. Assessment activity: "Winter Wildlife Inventory." (*Note:* An assessment activity is an enabling activity that involves student-teacher interaction and is designed to result in products or performances that can be used to assess student progress.) In cooperative groups, ask students to research and identify wildlife found in their community during the winter months. Then challenge students to hypothesize which of those organisms they believe impacts their local community the most, and why. Use an appropriate task (journal entry, concept web) and their hypotheses to assess students' acquisition of knowledge and assess Research and Continuity and Change using 1.19 checklist and 4.5 checklist.
3. Invite a local expert as guest speaker to speak on the winter ecology of their community.
4. Assessment activity: "Local Species Research." Ask students to research an individual species of winter wildlife, putting special emphasis on the organism's habitat and winter adaptation strategies. Then challenge students to create a Wildlife Community Map of the species the students researched. Use their research reports and maps to assess acquisition of knowledge, anecdotally assess application of knowledge learned in previous lessons, and assess Sustainability and Teamwork using 3.9 rubric and 3.10 rubrics.
5. Assessment activity: "The Mysteries of Adaptation." In cooperative groups ask students to synthesize what they've learned from their research on winter adaptation and their Wildlife Community Map and hypothesize why certain organisms (wolves, caribou, catamounts, woodland bison) that once lived nearby are no longer present. Use their hypotheses to assess students' application of knowledge learned in previous lessons and assess Continuity and Change and Movements and Settlements using 4.5 checklist and 6.8 rubric.
6. Revisit KWL and culminating activity checklist.

Week 3

Our Community's Winter Cultural Heritage

1. Revisit the Fall Strand's brainstorm list and review words and ideas that reflect the present-day cultural heritage of their community. Anecdotally assess the students' understanding of the term *culture* and the difference between cultural and natural heritage.
2. Assessment activity: "Life in Winter: A Local Photo Essay." Challenge students to develop, in cooperative groups, a photo essay that reflects their community's contemporary winter culture. Use their photo essays to assess students' acquisition of knowledge and assess Research and Teamwork using 1.19 checklist and 3.10 rubrics.
3. Invite a local expert as guest speaker to speak on the cultural heritage of their community.
4. Assessment activity: "Winter in the Old Days Scrapbook." Ask students to research past local cultural heritage, create a scrapbook that tells their ancestors' story of winter life, and, using a Venn diagram, compare and contrast the ways in which their ancestors and contemporaries adapted to winter. Use their scrapbooks, research reports, and a Venn diagrams to assess acquisition and application of knowledge and assess Continuity and Change using 4.5 checklist.
5. Revisit Winter Calendar task.

Week 4

Winter Survival and Adaptation

1. Preassessment task: Ask students to review their Wildlife Community Map, photo essays, and scrapbooks and begin writing a local winter survival tale. Use their first drafts to assess existing knowledge, affect, and application of knowledge learned in previous lessons.
2. Review with students the interviewing process (see Step 3, page 65).
3. Assessment activity: "Elder Interviews." Ask students to interview community elders (e.g., neighbor, grandparent, historical society referral) and document their winter survival tales. Have students share these stories with the class and compare and contrast with what they wrote in their first drafts. Anecdotally assess application of knowledge learned in previous lessons and assess Sustainability and Movements and Settlements using 3.9 rubric and 6.8 rubric.
4. Assessment activity: "Winter Survival Tales." Ask students to continue developing their tales. Use their tales to assess students' acquisition and application of knowledge from previous lessons.
5. Revisit KWL and culminating activity checklist.

Week 5

The Wisdom of Our Elders

1. Community partnership: Work with students on identifying community elders willing to share with students their wisdom and expertise in traditional knowledge and skills pertaining to winter adaptation and survival.
2. Meet with interested elders and help them prepare for their role in this school-community project, beginning with those elders interested in teaching the students quilting (see Step 4, page 75).

3. Assessment activity: "Community Quilting Bee." Invite those elders (and others) to a community quilting bee in which elders, students (cooperative groups), and community members collaborate in designing and creating quilts that reflect their local, past, and present natural and cultural winter heritage. Use the quilts to assess students' application of knowledge from previous lessons and assess Teamwork using 3.10 rubrics.
4. Assessment activity: "Researching Traditional Skills of Our Ancestors." In cooperative groups ask students to conduct initial research and write a report on a traditional winter adaptation skill of their choice which they want to experience through apprenticeship with one of the participating elders. Anecdotally assess affect and assess Research and Sustainability using 1.19 checklist and 3.9 rubric.
5. Revisit culminating activity checklist.

Week 6

Traditional Winter Survival Skills and Knowledge

1. Assessment activity: "Apprenticeships." Ask students as they participate in a one week apprenticeship to maintain a daily log documenting what they learn, discoveries they make, questions they have, and approaches they might take to pass this traditional winter skill on to future generations, and why. Then challenge students to design an investigation around their particular winter skill to test a particular question such as how this skill originated, why this skill was necessary, why this skill is or isn't still practiced, how and why this skill could be beneficial today, how this skill can be improved. Use students' logs and elder conferences to assess student affect, acquisition of knowledge, and project success, and assess Investigation using 7.2 rubric and video documentation.
2. Assessment activity: "Master Teachers." In cooperative groups ask students to plan, organize, and conduct a peer apprenticeship for the craft they've learned. Anecdotally assess affect, use elder conferences and videotaped presentations to assess knowledge acquisition, and assess Movements and Settlements using 6.8 rubric.

Week 7

Traditional Winter Survival Skills and Knowledge

1. Repeat week six with a second apprenticeship.
2. Revisit culminating activity checklist.

Week 8

Culminating Activity

1. Assessment activity: "Cabin Wellness: A Community Celebration." In cooperative groups ask students to complete a culminating project for the winter strand of their "Our Community's Story" unit. Remind students to continue to refer to their culminating activity checklist as they design their final demonstrations of sense of place. Videotape the culminating celebration for assessment and documentary purposes.
2. Postassessment. Conduct a final assessment of student progress using the Culminating Activity Checklist, standards 1.19, 3.9, 3.10, 4.5, 6.8, 7.2 rubrics/checklists, Winter Calendar task, and unit KWL.
3. Unit assessment: Using the "Unit Assessment Form" (see page 179), postassess the Winter Strand portion of the unit before planning and beginning the Spring Strand.

Appendix A

Local History Starter Kit

Local History IQ Test

1. What is the earliest known evidence of human beings living in your community?

2. What food crops did the first homesteaders grow? What was their diet?

3. In what year was your town or village charter signed?

4. What is the oldest building in your community?

5. How many farms are there in your community?

6. Name the three major industries in your town today; 100 years ago; 200 years ago.

7. List the three most significant dates or events that shaped the course of your community's history.

8. List three things that your community is known for historically.

9. How does your community reflect the cultural traditions of the United States? What contribution has your community made to U.S. and world history?

10. Retell a story you know about your community.

59 Curriculum Ideas for Teaching Local History

1. Local History IQ Test
2. Cemetery research and tombstone rubbings
3. Local Jeopardy game (see page 130, Sample Activity & Lesson Plan 11)
4. Local history certification
5. Local history CD-ROM: "Our Town"
6. Mural project: "Our Town Over Time"
7. Pioneers: People, places, and events that had the greatest influence on our community
8. Timeline of outstanding events: A guide to the most extraordinary events
9. Technology timelines and respective community change
10. Time capsules
11. Oral histories
12. Mentoring with area elders on age-old knowledge and skills
13. Town motto contest based on historical research
14. Community or school museum of artifacts, such as photos, diaries, clothing
15. Architecture research and community tours
16. Homesteads of old
17. Scale model of community
18. Local vocabulary
19. Archeological digs
20. Dramatic reenactments of important local events, such as founders' meetings, natural disasters, planning of major projects
21. Dancing through time
22. Music and song
23. Festivals or special events, such as a craft festival
24. Gallery of student artwork, for example, paintings and photos of elders
25. Writing poetry
26. Keeping diaries or journals; studying journals and letters from the past
27. Discovering your niche in the community
28. Envisioning the future
29. History of mental illness or poverty
30. Medicine, health, diet: local doctors, nurses, herbalists, and healers
31. Helping hands over time
32. Seasons of giving: seasonal community giving programs to restore our links to the past
33. Local fire department, its history and evolution
34. Local government, such as town meeting
35. Sports and recreation
36. Entertainment
37. Clothing, fashion, and style
38. Industry, business, and trade
39. Religion/church: local songbook
40. Video/big book library of living history
41. A guide to our community heritage
42. Who's who guide of community elders and the skills they have to share
43. Storybooks of days gone by
44. Weekly storytellers organized by topic and theme, such as by decade (the 1960s, 1970s)
45. Newspapers: report local news, both current and historical

46. Cookbook of local traditional and indigenous recipes
47. Breads through the ages
48. Historic gardens (with interviews, traditional skills, recipes, and food crops)
49. Home gardens
50. Food preservation
51. Seed-saving heirloom history
52. Foraging
53. Working landscape
54. Human impact on the land: relationship of different settlements to the land
55. Humans and animals: how different species have been perceived and used through history
56. Local traditions and history of trapping, hunting, fishing
57. Ancient trees, interview trees
58. Reading the landscape: an interview with a stone wall
59. Evolution of land-use permits

Appendix B

Forms, Rubrics, and Checklists

Checklist for *Getting to Know You*

Following is a short checklist to assist teachers in generating a list of topics and questions for a local history curriculum.

1. List local history topics or themes.

2. List a few focus questions to help define a local history learning project.

Following are examples of questions.

Land

What first attracted people to settle in your area? How has that changed over time?

People

Is there any evidence of indigenous settlements?

Who were the first European settlers?

Culture

How did the first inhabitants of your are survive? (food, shelter, clothing)

What rituals did they practice?
How has this changed over time?

What traditional skills and crafts from the past are still practiced in your community today?

What families have had a significant influence on your community?

Turning Points

What historical event were most important in shaping your community?

Focus Questions:

3. **List local resources** (organizations, people).

   Names of organizations *(historical societies, senior centers, libraries)*

   Names, addresses, and phone numbers of people *(elders, local historians, geologists)*

KWL Form

Name ______________________ **Date** ________

Activity ______________________

What I Know	What I Want to Know or Know More About	What I Learned

UNIT ASSESSMENT FORM (*Sample*)

1. Tally the number of times your unit addressed and you assessed your embedded standards.

Embedded Standard	**Addressed**	**Assessed**

2. Tally the various ways in which student performance in each embedded standard was assessed.

Embedded Standard	**Activity**	**Task**	**Tool**

3. Which embedded standards do you feel your unit needs to further address and you need to further assess and why?

4. In addition to the embedded standards, what other standards does your unit address?

5. Which multiple intelligences does your unit accommodate and what interdisciplinary connections does it provide?

6. Describe the balance your unit provides between qualitative assessment and quantitative evaluation.

Listening Checklist: Standard 1.13

Students listen actively and respond to communications.

Name ______________________________ **Date** __________

Activity ______________________________

_______ **Exhibits active listening skills**

- _______ maintains appropriate body language
- _______ is attentive
- _______ maintains eye contact
- _______ waits turn to respond

_______ **Able to restate or retell what has been said**

_______ **Asks related questions when interacting with speaker**

_______ **Asks clarifying questions when needed**

_______ **Demonstrates aural recall during follow-up activities**

Additional observations/comments:

TASK-SPECIFIC INTERVIEWING CHECKLIST

Below is an example of a task-specific interviewing checklist that could be used to assess a student's interviewing skills. Note that the criteria stated on this checklist are specific to interviewing and the particular interviewing activity in which the student is participating. Assessment tools such as this checklist can be an effective way to document student progress in specific skills, particularly performance skills in which progress can otherwise only be documented and then assessed through anecdotal observation or a video or tape recording.

Name ______________________________ **Date** __________

Activity ______________________________

Review the criteria below with your students before proceeding to the interviewing activity. Following the activity, you can confer with students individually and fill in the checklist together, or you can fill in a checklist independently and then compare and contrast your respective assessments.

_____ **Interviewer appeared prepared and organized**

_____ **Purpose of the interview was obvious**

_____ **Interviewer demonstrated active listening skills**

_____ **Interviewer posed questions in a logical and continuous sequence**

_____ **Interviewer was open to going with the flow of the interview**

_____ **Interviewer demonstrated respect toward the interviewee and the interviewee's opinions**

Additional observations/comments:

HERITAGE BRAINSTORM SORT (*Sample Task*)

Name ______________________________ **Date** __________

Activity ______________________________

Our Community's Natural Heritage	Our Community's Cultural Heritage
the brook	the playhouse
the common	the common
mountains	the courthouse
the park	the general store
animals	farming

Information Technology Rubric: Standard I.18

Students use computers, telecommunications, and other tools of technology to research, gather information and ideas, and represent information and ideas accurately and appropriately.

Name ______________________ **Date** __________ **Activity** ______________________

Good Start	Almost There	Got It!	Wow!
Uses a variety of sources when searching for information	and gathers and uses information and ideas form a variety of sources	and uses various tools of technology to organize and represent gathered information	and accurately and appropriately represents gathered information ideas

RESEARCH CHECKLIST: STANDARD 1.19

Students use organizational systems to obtain information from various sources, including libraries and the Internet.

Name ______________________________ **Date** __________

Activity ______________________________

Please check the organizational systems used in preparing this project.

_____ **Library Resources**

- _____ Card catalogue
- _____ *Readers' Guide to Periodicals*
- _____ Indices (such as the one for *National Geographic*)
- _____ Microfilm/microfiche
- _____ Video/filmstrip archives
- _____ Other: __________

_____ **Computer Resources**

- _____ Internet
- _____ Informational software (such as Encarta)
- _____ E-mail
- _____ Other: __________

_____ **Others:** __________

PROBLEM-SOLVING CHECKLIST: STANDARD 2.2

Students use reasoning strategies, knowledge, and common sense to solve complex problems related to all fields of knowledge.

Name ______________________ **Date** __________

Activity ______________________

Below is a list of some key strategies that can be used to solve problems. Check those you/your group used while performing the task you just completed.

_____ **Made observations of the situation**

_____ **Discussed and/or listed probable causes and effects of the situation**

_____ **Made connections between this situation and others that are similar**

_____ **Looked for patterns within this situation and/or between this situation and others that are similar**

_____ **Generated questions to help trigger ideas**

_____ **Generated hypotheses and discussed possible solutions**

_____ **Used process of elimination to help work toward a solution**

_____ **Got ideas and information from other sources (friends, teachers, books, etc.)**

_____ **Tested different approaches at solving the problem**

_____ **Made adjustments along the way**

_____ **Used drawings or objects to model or act out the problem**

_____ **Used numbers or formulas to help solve the problem**

_____ **Considered and investigated more than one solution to the problem**

Other strategies used:

Additional observations/comments:

Sustainability Rubric: Standard 3.9

Students make decisions that demonstrate understanding of natural and human communities, the ecological, economic, political, or social systems within them, and awareness of how their personal and collective actions affect the sustainability of these interrelated systems.

Name ____________________ **Date** __________ **Activity** ____________________

	Good Start	Almost There	Got It!	Wow!
Understanding Systems	Defines and gives examples of systems (e.g., ecosystems)	and identifies the individual parts of systems and explains how those parts work together to sustain their respective systems	and identifies internal and external influences (e.g., ecological, economic, social, and political) on systems and the limits those influences place on those systems	and identifies interactions between systems and the limitations those interactions place on those systems

SUSTAINABILITY RUBRIC: STANDARD 3.9 (continued)

Name ______________________ **Date** __________ **Activity** ______________________

	Good Start	Almost There	Got It!	Wow!
Understanding Personal Impact and Making Decisions	Recognizes direct impacts humans have on ecosystems and the environment	and recognizes both positive and negative impacts humans have on ecosystems and the environment	and identifies both direct and indirect short-term impacts humans have on the sustainability of ecosystems and the environment; personal decisions/actions clearly reflect consideration of those impacts	and identifies both direct and indirect long-term impacts humans have on the sustainability of ecosystems and the environment; personal decisions/actions clearly reflect consideration of those impacts

Teamwork Rubric: Standard 3.10

Students perform effectively on teams that set and achieve goals, conduct investigations, solve problems, and create solutions (e.g., by using consensus-building and cooperation to work toward group decisions.)

Name ______________ **Date** ________ **Activity** ______________

	Good Start	Almost There	Got It!	Wow!
Giving it my all and being responsible	Attempts to stay on task but struggles	Is focused on the task some of the time	Is focused on the task most of the time	Is focused on the task the whole time
Giving it my all and doing my share	Passively contributes (pays attention but lets others do all the work)	Occasionally contributes	Frequently contributes	Continuously contributes
Working with others, cooperating and collaborating	Only rarely follows group rules and systems	Sometimes follows group rules and systems	Always follows group rules and systems	Always follows group rules and systems
Getting the job done, compromising and resolving conflict	Attempts to accept group decision but struggles to not further argue personal points	Usually accepts group decision without further arguing personal points	Always accepts group decision without further arguing personal points	Always accepts and lends support to group decisions

TEAMWORK GROUP RUBRIC: STANDARD 3.10 (*continued*)

Name ____________________ **Date** __________ **Activity** ____________________

	Good Start	Almost There	Got It!	Wow!
Giving it our all (responsibility and productivity)	Attempts to stay on task, but struggles	Stays on task some of the time	Stays on task most of the time	Stays on task and is fully engaged the whole time
Valuing one another (acceptance, respect, and tolerance)	Some group members' ideas are respected and discussed	Most group members' ideas are respected and discussed	All group members' ideas are equally respected and discussed	All group members' ideas are equally respected, discussed, and in some way incorporated into final product
Working together (cooperation)	Most attempt to contribute but work is primarily done by one	Most contribute and participate constructively	All contribute and participate constructively	All continuously contribute and participate constructively
Getting the job done (compromise and conflict resolution)	Some unresolved conflict prevents task completion	Group agrees on most things but is still unable to fully complete tasks	Group agrees on most things, completes tasks, but some conflicts remain unresolved	Group arrives at decisions agreeably through consensus or majority and complete tasks smoothly

COMMUNITY SERVICE CHECKLIST: STANDARD 4.1

Students take an active role in their community.

Name ______________________ **Date** __________

Activity ______________________

_____ **Initiates an act of community service**

Example(s)

_____ **Responds to a call for community service**

Example(s)

_____ **Requests to perform an act of community service**

Example(s)

_____ **Uses strengths/talents to benefit the community**

Example(s)

_____ **Shares resources/materials to benefit the community**

Example(s)

_____ **Works collaboratively with members of the community**

Example(s)

Additional observations/comments:

Continuity and Change Checklist: Standard 4.5

Students understand continuity and change.

Name ______________________ **Date** __________

Activity ______________________

_____ **Recognizes examples of continuity**
Example(s)

____

_____ **Recognizes examples of change**
Example(s)

____

_____ **Recognizes and describes how new information and/or events led/lead to change**
Example(s)

____

_____ **Recognizes and describes alternating patterns of change**
Example(s)

____

_____ **Recognizes and describes continuous patterns of change**
Example(s)

____

_____ **Recognizes and describes cyclic patterns of change**
Example(s)

____

_____ **Recognizes and describes irregular patterns of change**
Example(s)

____

_____ **Recognizes when different audiences have different perceptions or opinions about a particular change**
Example(s)

____

Additional observations/comments:

Understanding Place Rubric: Standard 4.6

Students demonstrate understanding of the relationship between their local environment and community heritage and how each shapes their lives.

Name ______________________ **Date** __________ **Activity** ______________________

	Good Start	Almost There	Got It!	Wow!
Knowledge and Understanding	Identifies random elements of local community heritage (natural and/or cultural)	Identifies and explains how elements of both natural and cultural heritage shaped their community's historical development	Describes elements of local natural and cultural heritage for each historical period of their community's development from indigenous times to the present	Describes ways in which each historical period of their community's development has been influenced by the local natural and cultural heritage of preceding historical periods
Interrelationships	Identifies examples of natural heritage impacting cultural heritage and cultural heritage impacting natural heritage	Identifies and describes examples of the interactions between local natural and cultural heritage that shaped their community's development (heritage)	Identifies and explains the local natural and cultural heritage interactions of each historical period of their community's development from early times to the present	Identifies and explains how the natural and cultural interactions of one historical period impact the natural and cultural interactions of another
Personal Connections	Recognizes examples of personal connections they have with their community	Identifies examples of local community heritage that are impacting everyday life	Identifies and describes influences that both natural and cultural heritage have or have had on their personal life	Recognizes examples of the mutual impacts that their community heritage and their personal life have on another
Decision Making	Occasionally applies understanding of community heritage when making personal decisions	Generally applies understanding of community heritage when making personal decisions	Always applies understanding of community heritage when making personal decisions	Always applies understanding of community heritage (natural and cultural) when making both personal and public decisions
Community Relationship	Occasionally participates in community-related activities	Consistently participates in select community-related activities	Consistently participates in a variety of community-related activities	Consistently participates and, when possible, serves as leadership in a variety of community-related activities

Being a Historian Rubric: Standard 6.6

Students use historical methodology to make interpretations concerning history, change, and continuity.

Name ______________________ **Date** __________ **Activity** ______________________

	Good Start	**Almost There**	**Got It!**	**Wow!**
Historical Events/Eras	Names and describes historical events/eras	and places events/eras in chronological context	and identifies direct causes and effects related to events/eras	and identifies indirect causes and effects related to events/eras
Historical Change	Identifies examples of changes over time	and places examples of change in chronological context	and identifies direct causes and effects related to the changes	and identifies indirect causes and effects related to changes
Historical Continuity	Identifies examples of continuity over time	and places examples of continuity in chronological context	and identifies direct causes and effects related to examples of continuity	and identifies indirect causes and effects related to examples of continuity

Being a Historian Checklist: Standard 6.6 (*continued*)

Name ______________________________ **Date** __________

Activity ______________________________

_____ **Uses a variety of resources when researching and interpreting history, including:**

- _____ Primary documents (e.g., diaries, artifacts, photo archives, letters)
- _____ Oral history (e.g., storytelling, interviews)
- _____ Secondary sources (e.g., computer and library sources of written accounts)
- _____ Quantitative data (e.g., statistics, databases)

Movements and Settlements Rubric: Standard 6.8

Students analyze the factors and implications associated with the historical and contemporary movements and settlements of people and groups in various times in their local community, in Vermont, in the United States, and in various locations worldwide.

Name ______________________ **Date** __________ **Activity** ______________________

	Good Start	Almost There	Got It!	Wow!
Analyzes historical/ contemporary movements and settlements	Identifies examples of historical/contemporary movements and settlements	and explains factors (causes) that led to those historical/ contemporary movements and settlements	and explains the direct implications and long-term effects of those historical/contemporary movements and settlements	and explains patterns that exist between local and worldwide historical/ contemporary movements and settlements and the impacts these movements and settlements had on one another

Scientific Method, Observation Rubric: Standard 7.1

Name ____________________ **Date** __________ **Activity** ____________________

	Good Start	Almost There	Got It!	Wow!
Time and effort	Stops observing after making one or two observations	Stops observing after making several observations	Stops observing only after it becomes difficult to notice anything more	Continues observing even though isn't immediately finding anything more
Observing wholes as well as parts	Makes all of one type of observation and none of the other	Makes many more of one type of observation than the other	Makes slightly more of one type of observation than the other	Makes a balanced amount of both types of observations
Looking for similarities and differences	Understands the importance of looking for similarities and differences	Notices some similarities and differences	Deliberately looks for similarities and differences	Concentrates on looking for similarities and differences
Using all the senses applicable	Uses one sense	Uses more than one sense but primarily relies on one sense	Uses most of the senses equally	Uses a balance of all the senses
Looking for patterns	Understands the importance of looking for patterns	Happens to notice some patterns	Deliberately looks for patterns	Concentrates on finding patterns

Scientific Method, Questioning Rubric: Standards 7.1 and 2.1

Name ____________________ **Date** __________ **Activity** ____________________

	Good Start	Almost There	Got It!	Wow!
Time and effort	Asks some questions that come immediately to mind	Ask many questions that comes immediately to mind	Deliberately tries to come up with questions beyond those that come immediately to mind	Stops asking questions only when unable to come up with anything more to ask or until time runs out
Balance of different types of questions	Every question is a "just the facts please!" question	Most of the questions are "just the facts please!" questions	Some of the questions are "just the facts please!" questions	Asks a balance of different types of questions
	Every question is a "but why?" question	Most of the questions are "but why?" questions	Some of the questions are "but why?" questions	
	Every question is a "what if?" question	Most of the questions are "what if?" questions	Some of the questions are "what if?" questions	

Scientific Method, Hypothesizing Rubric: Standard 7.1

Name ______________________ Date __________ Activity ______________________

	Good Start	Almost There	Got It!	Wow!
Analyzing and applying evidence (existing data)	Considers a few pieces of data when formulating hypotheses	Considers several pieces of data when formulating hypotheses	Considers many pieces of data when formulating hypotheses	Considers every piece of data when formulating hypotheses
Applying existing knowledge	Applies a few things already known toward formulating hypotheses	Applies several things already known toward formulating hypotheses	Applies many things already known toward formulating hypotheses	Applies everything already known and recollected toward formulating hypotheses
Applying previous experience	Relates to a few previous experiences when formulating hypotheses	Relates to several previous experiences when formulating hypotheses	Relates to many previous experiences when formulating hypotheses	Relates every relevant previous experience that can be recalled when formulating hypotheses
Relating hypotheses to the problem/ question	Attempts to develop hypotheses that address the problem or question	Hypotheses somewhat or indirectly address the problem or question	Hypotheses address the problem or question	Hypotheses address the problem or question and include supporting evidence
Generating alternative hypotheses	Generates one hypothesis	Generates more than one hypothesis and one is extensively analyzed and supported	Generates more than one hypothesis and the majority are extensively analyzed and supported	Generates more than one hypothesis and all of them are extensively analyzed and supported

Scientific Method, Formulating Conclusions Rubric: Standard 7.1

Name ______________ **Date** ________ **Activity** ______________

Good Start	Almost There	Got It!	Wow!
Bases conclusions on observations and results	and uses all observations and results when formulating a conclusion	and defends and supports conclusions using observations and results; generates new questions from observations, results, and conclusions	and generates alternative conclusions and explanations; defends and supports conclusions using observations and results as well as other outside evidence; uses new questions raised from conclusions to determine next steps

Investigation Rubric: Standard 7.2

Students design and conduct a variety of their own investigations and projects.

Name ______________________ **Date** __________ **Activity** ____________________

	Good Start	Almost There	Got It!	Wow!
Investigating the question or problem	Attempts to design an investigation that addresses the question or problem	Experiment somewhat or indirectly addresses the question or problem	Experiment addresses the question or problem	Experiment addresses this and related questions or problems
Designing a fair and controlled experiment (test)	Experiment contains several unwanted variables that can be controlled	Experiment contains some unwanted variables that are hard to control	Experiment is as fair and controlled as possible, given the circumstances	Experiment is pure; no unwanted variables exist
Providing the necessary materials for constructing and conducting the experiment	Some necessary materials are missing and some are not appropriate for the experiment	All necessary materials are present but not all are appropriate for the experiment	All necessary materials are present and appropriate for the experiment	All necessary materials, as well as back-up or contingency supplies, are present and appropriate for the experiment
Planning and organizing the procedure for the experiment	Basic procedures are sequenced, but step-by-step details are lacking	Basic procedures are sequenced with some step-by-step details included	All procedures are sequenced and include detailed step-by-step directions	All procedures are sequenced and include step-by-step details along with diagrams
Systematically observing and collecting and recording an adequate amount of data	One or two observations and data collections are made and recorded	Several observations and data collections are made and recorded but not enough to validate the conclusion	A validating number of observation and data collections are made and recorded	A validating number of observations and data collections are made and recorded systematically

Measurement Checklist/Rubric: Standard 7.7

Students use geometric and measurement concepts.

Name ______________________ **Date** __________ **Activity** ______________________

Understanding measurement concepts

_____ Defines the term measurement; explains what measurement is

_____ Identifies situations involving or requiring measurement

_____ Distinguishes between the various dimensions of measurement (distance, speed, weight, volume, time)

	Good Start	Almost There	Got It!	Wow!
Use of measurement tools	Identifies conventional tools used for measuring distance, speed, weight, volume, and time	and chooses and correctly uses appropriate tool	and obtains accurate results and uses appropriate units when representing results	and uses alternative tools and approaches accurately

Systems Analysis Checklist: Standard 7.II

Students analyze and understand living and nonliving systems (e.g., biological, chemical, electrical, mechanical, optical) as collections of interrelated parts and interconnected systems.

______ **Defines and gives examples of systems**
Example(s)

______ **Distinguishes between a system and its parts**
Example(s)

______ **Distinguishes between living and nonliving systems and parts of systems**
Example(s)

______ **Explains the functions of particular systems**
Example(s)

______ **Explains the functions of the parts of particular systems**
Example(s)

______ **Recognizes and explains how a system's parts interconnect**
Example(s)

______ **Recognizes and explains how different systems interconnect**
Example(s)

______ **Identifies inputs needed to maintain/sustain particular systems**
Example(s)

______ **Identifies outputs generated by particular systems**
Example(s)

______ **Demonstrates understanding of the limitations of particular systems**
Example(s)

______ **Demonstrates understanding of working systems (parts, inputs, processes, outputs) through models, simulations, diagrams, etc. (samples attached)**
Example(s)

Additional observations/comments:

Organisms Rubric: Standard 7.13

Students understand the characteristics of organisms, see patterns of similarity and differences among living organisms, understand the role of evolution, and recognize the interdependence of all systems that support life.

Name ____________ **Date** ________ **Activity** ____________

Good Start	Almost There	Got It!	Wow!
Identifies characteristics and structures that are similar and different between organisms Categorizes organisms based on their similar and different characteristics and structures	and uses characteristics and structures to accurately identify and classify organisms	and explains the functions of an organism's characteristics and structures and how they distinguish that organism from others	and recognizes and explains how specific characteristics and structures play a part in an organism's time, place, and role (niche) within a habitat or ecosystem.

Interdependence Rubric: Standard 7.13

Students understand the characteristics of organisms, see patterns of similarity and differences among living organisms, understand the role of evolution, and recognize the interdependence of all systems that support life.

Name ______________________ **Date** __________ **Activity** ____________________

Good Start	Almost There	Got It!	Wow!
Understands the difference between and identifies both short- and long-term influences/consequences	and understands the difference between and recognizes both direct (linear) and indirect (complex) relationships	and identifies both the positive and negative impacts of any one phenomenon	and naturally recognizes and distinguishes wholes and parts

Glossary

Assessment Ongoing monitoring of student or program performance and gathering of qualitative information on student or program progress.

Cultural Literacy An extensive, internalized understanding of the literature, lore, common stories, traditional crafts and skills, religious beliefs, and folkways of our recent and distant past. A way of being that reflects a deep, internalized understanding of local culture and the importance of preserving local community and cultural uniqueness.

Culturally Responsive Curricula Curricula that accommodate and incorporate those unique characteristics of the local community that are relevant to and directly impact and influence the students of that community.

Ecological Literacy An extensive, internalized understanding of systems and the basic ecological principles that impact all systems; a way of being that embodies that understanding.

Evaluation The quantitative categorizing of a student's or program's overall performance and success.

Living Traditions Cultural heritage. The community-based skills, stories, knowledge, and crafts passed along from culture to culture, generation to generation.

Natural Heritage The elements of our environment, such as the landscape, soil, waterways, weather, climate, flora, and fauna, that historically influenced and presently impact our culture and cultural heritage.

Pedagogy The art and science of teaching. The overall approach (mission, goals, objectives, content, skills, methods, assessment, and evaluation) to teaching that evolves as a manifestation of the particular philosophy and beliefs held by the educator.

Place-Based Curriculum A curriculum that utilizes a community's resources, history, and local uniqueness to teach essential skills and concepts that stimulate discovery of the broader world. An interdisciplinary curriculum woven from the threads of local cultural and natural heritage.

Service-Learning Community-based work that has a built-in educational component, such as students growing food and preparing meals at a local soup kitchen to meet learning standards in food and nutrition for a science class.

Social Ecology A holistic study that reacquaints people with their natural heritage through an integrated study of the interrelationships between human and natural systems.

Professional Development Courses and Workshops

Join our growing network of schools and communities creating a living curriculum that stimulates the natural curiosity of children to explore the world around them.

Courses, Workshops, and Mentorships

- **Three-Credit Courses**
Developing integrated units focusing on assessment-based instruction using the natural environment and surrounding community for learning about the wider world.
- **Workshops and After-School Seminars**
Content-specific projects and activities aligned to state learning standards
- **Lead Teacher Mentorships**
Ongoing professional development in the classroom

Our class on standards and assessment has been the clearest and most informative of all I have attended, and I've attended a lot of them. The staff at Food Works are Master Teachers and bring with them an enthusiasm that is contagious.

—Judy LeBlanc, Principal, Troy School, North Troy, Vermont

Content Strands

All our courses, workshops and mentorships focus on standards-based curriculum development combining three major content strands, according to the needs of each school's teaching staff:

- **Agricultural Literacy**
Learning the agricultural story of your community
- **Ecological Literacy**
Studying the natural cycles of the living world
- **Cultural Literacy**
Understanding the traditions and historical development of the local community and documenting local history

Undeniably the most thought-provoking, informative, stimulating, and academic course I have encountered so far in my professional career of teaching.

—Dana Pramuk, 5th Grade Teacher, Rochester Elementary School, Rochester, Vermont

Possible Content Areas

- Growing historic theme gardens and building outdoor bread ovens
- Developing seasonal units exploring and modeling the local watershed
- Designing interdisciplinary projects around community-wide celebrations

Plus nature trails, schoolyard habitats, and much, much more

To arrange for a course or workshop in your school, please call: (802) 223-1515 or 1-800-310-1515 (outside Vermont) or e-mail: foodwork@together.net

One-Day Workshop	**$600 plus travel (in Vermont)**
Three-Credit Professional Development Course	**$690 per teacher**

GUIDEBOOKS FROM COMMON ROOTS PRESS

Thousands of educators around the country are using our path-breaking guidebooks. Are you?

NEW!

LASTING RESULTS

Rediscovering the Promise of Standards Through Assessment-Based Instruction

Complete with user-friendly assessment activities, tasks, and tools (scoring guides such as rubrics and checklists), **Lasting Results** is a ready reference for teachers, curriculum coordinators, and administrators interested in aligning their own curricula to state and national educational standards through assessment-based instruction.

paper; 8.5 x 11; comb binding; 176 pages; illustrations; forms, rubrics, checklists; resources
$24.95; ISBN: 1-884430-05-8

When I first show teachers Lasting Results, *they inevitably remark, "This is just what I need!" I'm finding the teachers who use it find they finally have a good guide for making the transition from standards-linked to standards-aligned instruction.*

—Linda Wellings, School Program Director, Shelburne Farms, Vermont

NEW!

LIVING TRADITIONS

Teaching Local History Using State and National Learning Standards

Living Traditions guides teachers through a clear, step-by-step process for developing integrated, standards-based curricula focusing on the stories, crafts, and traditions of the community that surrounds their school. Part II is a complete, ready-to-use seasonal unit of place-based projects and learning activities that can be undertaken in any community and aligned to any state's or school district's educational standards.

paper; 8.5 x 11; 240 pages; b&w photos and illustrations; activities; forms, rubrics, checklists; glossary; appendixes; resources $19.95; ISBN: 1-884430-06-6

Living Traditions *creates a whole new dimension for exploring authentic, language-rich stories encouraging students to explore personal topics of interest in their own writing.*

—Newton Baker, 4th Grade Teacher, Union Elementary School, Montpelier, Vermont

While this guide serves primarily as a tool for teachers, it is also a call to action to the wider general public for educating the next generation to honor and learn about our natural and cultural heritage, and the living traditions that go along with it.

—from the Foreword by U.S. Senator Patrick Leahy

DIGGING DEEPER

Integrating Youth Gardens into Schools and Communities

A comprehensive guide and invaluable resource for educators and parents that contains dozens of project ideas for the curious child out in the garden and in nature. Much more than a how-to manual on growing food with children, **Digging Deeper** demonstrates how well-planned gardening programs can become the foundation for building community-based schools for lifelong learning.

paper; 8.5 x 11; 160 pages; b&w photos and illustrations; activities; appendixes $19.95; ISBN: 1-884430-04-X

A cornucopia of practical ideas for educators interested in making learning come to life for their students.

—Dr. Mark Hull, former State of Vermont Commissioner of Education

Digging Deeper *is a must for those ready to make a serious commitment to organizing and coordinating youth garden programs. It offers a wealth of information, from garden development and construction guidelines, to seasonal events and learning activities.*

—Judy Sims, Elementary Teacher and Youth Garden Coordinator, Monta Vista Elementary School, California

THE INDOOR RIVER BOOK

This first-of-its-kind teacher's guide details a simple step-by-step process for building an indoor aquatic habitat modeled after the local watershed, adaptable for teachers with little or no experience in environmental activities in school.

paper; 8.5 x 11; 144 pages; b&w photos and illustrations; activities; appendixes; resources $14.95; ISBN: 0-7872-3602-0

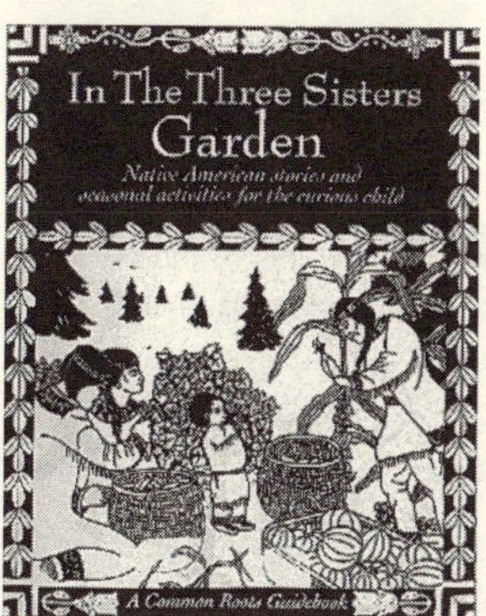
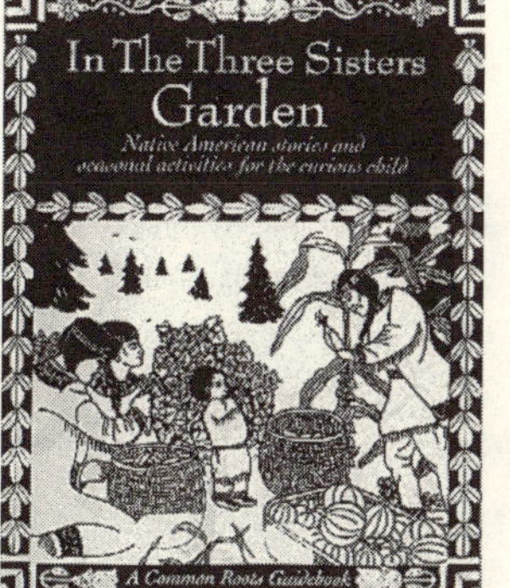

IN THE THREE SISTERS GARDEN

Sister Corn, Sister Bean and Sister Squash introduce children to gardening in two distinct yearlong adventures that explore the ancient wisdom of the land.

paper; 8.5 x 11; 384 pages; illustrations; activities; bibliography; index; resources $28.95; ISBN: 0-7872-2175-9

THE WONDERFUL WORLD OF WIGGLERS

Integrated hands-on activities and projects help children to understand the crucial relationships between earthworms, the soil and ecological sustainability.

paper; 8.5 x 11; 168 pages; illustrations; activities; bibliography; appendix $14.95; ISBN: 1-884430-00-7

EXPLORING THE SECRETS OF THE MEADOW-THICKET

Children are guided on seasonal journeys filled with stories, activities, and adventures involving animals, bugs, grasses, bushes, and trees.

paper; 8.5 x 11; 256 pages; illustrations; activities; bibliography; resources $18.95; ISBN: 1-884430-02-3

EXPLORING THE FOREST WITH GRANDFOREST TREE

Grandforest Tree, who is very old and very wise, spins tales of the forest progressing through the seasons with many opportunities for outdoor and indoor activities and mysteries to solve.

paper; 8.5 x 11; 272 pages; illustrations; activities; bibliography; resources $18.95; ISBN: 1-884430-03-1

Instructional Videos

GETTING TO KNOW YOU

Learning from the Wisdom of Our Elders

Accompanying the teacher's guidebook *Living Traditions*, **Getting to Know You** demonstrates the eight-step process for developing and implementing local service-learning curriculum, with a special focus on elders as the carriers of traditional knowledge and age-old wisdom.

Running time: 35 mins.
Cost: $19.95

NEW!

WHERE RIVERS MEET

A Students' History of Montpelier

This unique historical documentary, created by elementary-aged students, is the first complete documentary on the history of Vermont's capital city.

Where Rivers Meet follows the step-by-step process of a group of student researchers uncovering their city's history as they interview local elders and historians, take a historic walking tour of Montpelier, discover old photographs and archival materials at the state historical library, and display and present their findings on an indoor river diorama of the city that they built themselves.

Including rare archival photos and anecdotes on the founding and development of America's smallest state capital, **Where Rivers Meet** is an excellent guide demonstrating how students can research and document their community's history in a powerful, hands-on way.

Running time: 28 mins.
Cost: $19.95

COMMON ROOTS

A School's Journey

Highlights the process of a K–8 school refocusing its entire curriculum around the natural and cultural history of the surrounding town, beginning with gardens and nature trails.

Running time: 28 mins.
Cost: $19.95

Guidebook and Video Order Form

To order books and videos, call toll free: 1-800-310-1515, e-mail Food Works at foodwork@together.net, or mail or fax the following form to:

Food Works
Common Roots Press
64 Main Street
Montpelier, VT 05602
Fax: (802) 229-5277

Name ______________________

Address ______________________

City, State, Zip ______________________

Daytime Phone ______________________

E-mail ______________________

Guidebooks	Price	Quantity	Total
Living Traditions	$19.95	______	______
Lasting Results	$24.95	______	______
Digging Deeper	$19.95	______	______
The Indoor River Book	$14.95	______	______
In The Three Sisters Garden	$28.95	______	______
The Wonderful World of Wigglers	$14.95	______	______
Exploring the Secrets of the Meadow-Thicket	$18.95	______	______
Exploring the Forest with Grandforest Tree	$18.95	______	______
Instructional Videos			
Where Rivers Meet	$19.95	______	______
Getting to Know You	$19.95	______	______
Common Roots	$19.95	______	______

Total books/videos ordered ______